MAUREEN LENNON

Maureen is a Hull-based writer, and a graduate from the English and Theatre Studies BA at the University of Bristol and the Writing for Performance and Publication MA at the University of Leeds. She is a Leeds Playhouse FUSE writer 2019, a Sphinx30 playwright and a BBC's Voices 2024 writer. In 2020, her play *Helen* was shortlisted for the Theatre503 International Playwriting Prize.

Her full-length plays include *Baby He Loves You* (Middle Child, 2024), *Dead Girls Rising* (Silent Uproar, 2024), *Guts! The Musical* (Hull Truck Theatre, 2024), *Helen* (Theatre503 and Terrain Theatre, 2023), *The Coppergate Woman* (York Theatre Royal, 2022), *Us Against Whatever* (Middle Child Theatre, 2019) and *Bare Skin On Briny Waters* (Bellow Theatre and Hull City of Culture, 2017). She has also written work for Paines Plough, Sheffield Theatres and Pilot Theatre.

As well as work for theatre she has written for Hull Truck's online soap opera *Consequences*, Middle Child Theatre's online animated panto, *Miracle on the Humber* – a series of short films produced by Hull Truck and KCOM, and *Virtual Horizons* – a VR theatre experience. She was a BoxFresh selected writer in 2023 and worked with Box of Tricks and Rope Ladder Fiction on their pilot scheme.

Other Titles in this Series

Josh Azouz
BUGGY BABY
GIGI & DAR
THE MIKVAH PROJECT
ONCE UPON A TIME IN NAZI OCCUPIED
  TUNISIA
VICTORIA'S KNICKERS

Ellen Brammar
MODEST

Chris Bush
THE ASSASSINATION OF KATIE HOPKINS
  with Matt Winkworth
THE CHANGING ROOM
CHRIS BUSH PLAYS: ONE
A DOLL'S HOUSE after Ibsen
FAUSTUS: THAT DAMNED WOMAN
HUNGRY
JANE EYRE after Brontë
THE LAST NOËL
OTHERLAND
ROCK/PAPER/SCISSORS
ROBIN HOOD AND THE CHRISTMAS HEIST
STANDING AT THE SKY'S EDGE
  with Richard Hawley
STEEL

Billie Collins
PEAK STUFF
TOO MUCH WORLD AT ONCE

Phoebe Eclair-Powell
DORIAN after Oscar Wilde
EPIC LOVE AND POP SONGS
FURY
HARM
SHED: EXPLODED VIEW
WINK

Calum Finlay
FANNY

Beth Flintoff
THE BALLAD OF MARIA MARTEN
THE GLOVE THIEF
REBELLIOUS WOMEN

Natasha Gordon
NINE NIGHT

Lucy Kirkwood
BEAUTY AND THE BEAST
  with Katie Mitchell
BLOODY WIMMIN
THE CHILDREN
CHIMERICA
HEDDA after Ibsen
THE HUMAN BODY
IT FELT EMPTY WHEN THE HEART
  WENT AT FIRST BUT IT IS
  ALRIGHT NOW
LUCY KIRKWOOD PLAYS: ONE
MOSQUITOES
NSFW
RAPTURE
TINDERBOX
THE WELKIN

Maureen Lennon
HELEN

Liz Lochhead
BLOOD AND ICE
DRACULA after Stoker
EDUCATING AGNES ('The School for Wives')
  after Molière
GOOD THINGS
LIZ LOCHHEAD: FIVE PLAYS
MARY QUEEN OF SCOTS GOT
  HER HEAD CHOPPED OFF
MEDEA after Euripides
MISERYGUTS ('The Miser')
  & TARTUFFE after Molière
PERFECT DAYS
THEBANS after Euripides & Sophocles
THON MAN MOLIÈRE

Evan Placey
BANANA BOYS
CONSENSUAL
GIRLS LIKE THAT
HOLLOWAY JONES
JEKYLL & HYDE after Robert Louis Stevenson
PETER PAN after J.M. Barrie
PRONOUN

Frances Poet
ADAM
FIBRES
GUT
MAGGIE MAY
STILL

Jessica Swale
BLUE STOCKINGS
THE JUNGLE BOOK after Rudyard Kipling
NELL GWYNN

debbie tucker green
BORN BAD
DEBBIE TUCKER GREEN PLAYS: ONE
DIRTY BUTTERFLY
EAR FOR EYE
HANG
NUT
A PROFOUNDLY AFFECTIONATE,
  PASSIONATE DEVOTION TO
  SOMEONE (– NOUN)
RANDOM
STONING MARY
TRADE & GENERATIONS
TRUTH AND RECONCILIATION

Phoebe Waller-Bridge
FLEABAG

Amanda Whittington
BE MY BABY
THE INVINCIBLES
KISS ME QUICKSTEP
LADIES' DAY
LADIES DOWN UNDER
LADIES UNLEASHED
MIGHTY ATOMS
SATIN 'N' STEEL
THE THRILL OF LOVE

Maureen Lennon

MARY AND THE HYENAS

*A musical vindication of
the life of Mary Wollstonecraft*

NICK HERN BOOKS
London
www.nickhernbooks.co.uk

A Nick Hern Book

Mary and the Hyenas first published in Great Britain as a paperback original in 2025 by Nick Hern Books Limited, The Glasshouse, 49a Goldhawk Road, London W12 8QP

Mary and the Hyenas copyright © 2025 Maureen Lennon

Maureen Lennon has asserted her right to be identified as the author of this work

Cover photography by Tom Arran

Designed and typeset by Nick Hern Books, London
Printed in Great Britain by Mimeo Ltd, Huntingdon, Cambridgeshire PE29 6XX

A CIP catalogue record for this book is available from the British Library

ISBN 978 1 83904 432 8

CAUTION All rights whatsoever in this play are strictly reserved. Requests to reproduce the text in whole or in part should be addressed to the publisher.

Amateur Performing Rights Applications for performance, including readings and excerpts, by amateurs in the English language should be addressed to the Performing Rights Department, Nick Hern Books, The Glasshouse, 49a Goldhawk Road, London W12 8QP, *tel* +44 (0)20 8749 4953, *email* rights@nickhernbooks.co.uk, except as follows:

Australia: ORiGiN Theatrical, *tel* +61 (2) 8514 5201, *email* enquiries@originmusic.com.au, *web* www.origintheatrical.com.au

New Zealand: Play Bureau, 20 Rua Street, Mangapapa, Gisborne 4010, *tel* +64 21 258 3998, *email* info@playbureau.com

United States and Canada: United Agents Ltd, as below

Professional Performing Rights Applications for performance by professionals in any medium and in any language throughout the world should be addressed to United Agents Ltd, 12–26 Lexington St, London W1F 0LE, *tel* +44 (0)20 3214 0800, *email* info@unitedagents.co.uk

No performance of any kind may be given unless a licence has been obtained. Applications should be made before rehearsals begin. Publication of this play does not necessarily indicate its availability for performance.

www.nickhernbooks.co.uk/environmental-policy

Nick Hern Books' authorised representative in the EU is
Easy Access System Europe – Mustamäe tee 50, 10621 Tallinn, Estonia
email gpsr.requests@easproject.com

For Mary.
For all of us.

Mary and the Hyenas was co-produced by Hull Truck Theatre and Pilot Theatre, and was first performed at Hull Truck Theatre on 7 February 2025. The production transferred to Wilton's Music Hall, London, on 18 March 2025. The cast was as follows:

MARY WOLLSTONECRAFT	Laura Elsworthy
ELIZA WOLLSTONECRAFT, DR PRICE, MARGARET KINGSBOROUGH, THÉROIGNE DE MÉRICOURT, FANNY IMLAY	Beth Crame
ELIZABETH WOLLSTONECRAFT, MIDWIFE, LADY KINGSBOROUGH, WILLIAM GODWIN, OLYMPE DE GOUGES	Kate Hampson
FANNY BLOOD, FUSELI, EDWARD WOLLSTONECRAFT, HELEN WILLIAMS	Kat Johns-Burke
MARY SHELLEY, THOMAS PAINE, MARGUERITE	Ainy Medina
DOCTOR, EVERINA WOLLSTONECRAFT, GILBERT IMLAY, JOSEPH JOHNSON	Elexi Walker

Director	Esther Richardson
Designer	Sara Perks
Music	Billy Nomates (Tor Maries)
Lyrics	Maureen Lennon
	& Billy Nomates (Tor Maries)
Lighting Designer	Chris Davey
Musical Director	Emily Levy
Sound Designer	Adam McCready
Movement Director	Ayesha Fazal
Assistant Director	Eliza Beth Stevens
Master Carpenter	Chris Bewers
Workshop Carpenters	Luke James
	Daniel Lewis
Scenic Artists	Sarah Feasey
	Natalie Young
Costume Supervisor	Siân Thomas
Costume Assistant	Molly Frankland
Company Stage Manager	Shona Wright
Deputy Stage Manager	Lily O'Connor
Assistant Stage Manager	Sarah Goodyear
Production Managers	Sarah Barton (Hull Truck Theatre)
	Luke James (Pilot Theatre)
Producer	Luke Dankoff (Hull Truck Theatre)
Executive Producer	Mandy Smith (Pilot Theatre)

Mary and the Hyenas was developed with the support of the National Theatre's Generate programme.

Characters

MARY WOLLSTONECRAFT

THE HYENAS: *The chorus, who sing and play all parts except Mary, including:*

MARY SHELLEY
FANNY IMLAY
FANNY BLOOD
ELIZA WOLLSTONECRAFT
EVERINA WOLLSTONECRAFT
ELIZABETH WOLLSTONECRAFT
EDWARD WOLLSTONECRAFT
MARGARET KINGSBOROUGH
MARGUERITE
GILBERT IMLAY
JOSEPH JOHNSON
DR PRICE
WILLIAM GODWIN
EDMUND BURKE
HENRY FUSELI
THOMAS PAINE
OLYMPE DE GOUGES
THÉROIGNE DE MÉRICOURT
HELEN WILLIAMS
MADAME ROLAND
LADY KINGSBOROUGH
THE KING
A DOCTOR
A PUPIL
A MIDWIFE
A STREET VENDOR
MEREDITH BISHOP

Casting does NOT need to be realistic but should feel playful, imaginative and reflect the diversity of identities that are oppressed by patriarchy.

Notes on the Text

/ indicates interruption.

– in place of a line indicates a pause.

– at the end of a line indicates a thought that can't be finished.

This text went to press before the end of rehearsals and so may differ slightly from the play as performed.

ACT ONE

A clock above gives us today's year: e.g. 2025.

MARY *on a bed, elevated, howling, on all-fours.*

MARY. AHHHHHHHHHHHHHHHHHHHHHHHHHHHHH.

　THE HYENAS *appear.*

HYENAS. The day Mary Wollstonecraft died a comet shot across the sky.

　The world stopped to look up.

　Nothing like that had been seen in a lifetime.

　It was like the future.

　The future was scorching ahead.

MARY. Aggghhhowwwwwld.

HYENAS. Hyena in petticoats. That was what they called her.

　We can't think why.

　But that's the thing about women born before their time.

　You wish they could be here now –

　To know how we would join them in their roars.

　So, this is the story of Mary

　Told for all women, who find themselves

　Howling at the world.

Maybe we have a hint of a howl. MARY*'s plinth descends. The clock suddenly rewinds. Landing on it is a date: 1797.*

One of THE HYENAS *steps forward and becomes the* MIDWIFE.

MARY. Ahhhhhhhhhhhhhhhhhhh. Now, surely now.

MIDWIFE. No.

MARY. YES.

MIDWIFE. NO.

MARY. It must be time to push.

MIDWIFE. Not yet. Breathe.

MARY. It's taking too long. With Fanny it was much quicker.

MIDWIFE. With fannies it often is.

MARY. What?

MIDWIFE. Maybe she had an instinct for it. Some babies do.

MARY. Ahhh. GOD.

MIDWIFE. Breathe. Breathing.

MARY. I AM breathing. I am clearly breathing.

FANNY. Mummy.

MARY looks up, sees FANNY peering from a doorframe. Tries to compose herself.

MARY. No, no, Fanny. Go downstairs.

FANNY. Mummy, what's wrong?

MARY. Nothing's wrong, darling, nothingahhhhhhh /

FANNY. Are they hurting you? Make them stop.

MIDWIFE. About nine months too late to stop.

MARY. Everything's fine, darling, ahh – GO back downstairs. Love. Love you.

FANNY goes. MARY curls up somewhere, maybe the bed, maybe a corner.

Oh God she's right, I don't want to do this any more make it stop.

MIDWIFE. Come on now, Mary.

MARY. I can't. I can't do it. I won't.

The MIDWIFE *goes to her, gets her up. Shakes her into shape.*

MIDWIFE. Yes you will, Mary Wollstonecraft.

MARY. No. Ahhh no please.

She begins to breathe heavily again, contraction approaching.

MIDWIFE. When I said I was to attend you there was some chat in my household you know. My husband said I heard she's got the mouth of a rabid dog, you better be on your mettle.

MARY. Is this meant to be making me feel better?

MIDWIFE. I heard she's a wild one. A hyena.

MARY. Because it is NOT.

MIDWIFE. I hear she's unnatural, demands the same for women as men, sets herself up in trousers as the leader of a household.

MARY. If I ever get hold of your husband I think he would regret taking such a florid tone.

MIDWIFE. And I said good. I said I can't wait to meet her. Author of *The Rights of Woman*. To go against all that. A battleaxe /

MARY. I'm actually very – a lot of it is me talking about how to give women better sensibilities. AHHHHHHHHHHHHHHHHHHHH. Fuuuuurig. (*She blows out.*) Cultivate our finer senses. Our intellect. Your husband might learn a lot from reading it /

MIDWIFE. Say fuck if you mean fuck. I mean if you can't when a head's coming out your gash then / well

MARY. As might you.

ACT ONE   13

MIDWIFE. What?

MARY. Learn something if you read it.

MIDWIFE. Can't read. Never had any need. You don't find no words in tuppences.

MARY. Ahhhhh. Please. Let. Me. Push.

MIDWIFE. I told him I want to meet the woman who wrote it though. Who caused such a fuss. Who said, 'Sod all them, and what they think and how they think the whole world might be.'

MARY. That's not exactly /

MIDWIFE. I want to meet the woman who said, 'We deserve more and I'm going to demand it.' Not just in mutterings and bitching round the washhouse. But out loud. Proper. Written down in words they had to take notice of.

MARY. I'm not sure they listened any more because it was written down.

MIDWIFE. They did. Why do you think they went at you so hard? Because they could tell you were marching into war and you was doing it in a way that frightened them.

MARY. Ahhhhhhhh. God. Help. Me.

MIDWIFE. Never mind God. You. You was the one I was excited to meet. I said I can't wait to see how she does battle.

MARY *is panting hard. Blowing. Suddenly the* MIDWIFE *is underneath and between her legs. She knows it is nearly time.*

So come on.

MARY. What?

MIDWIFE. Show me. Do battle, Mary. Now.

MARY. Ahh no /

MIDWIFE. Now /

MARY. I don't /

MIDWIFE. It's time. PUSH.

MARY. Oh thank God.

MIDWIFE. Push, come on.

MARY. I. Am. Pushing.

MIDWIFE. Push harder.

MARY. Ahhhhhhh. YOU push harder.

MIDWIFE. NOW.

MARY. AHHHHHHHHHHHHHHHHHHHHHHHHHHHHHH. FUCK.

A baby slithers out. Slimy and bloody and shitty and weak and slithery.

MIDWIFE. You've done it.

MARY. And he's well? He's breathing.

MARY *is scrambling to turn around. The* MIDWIFE *is holding the baby. Tapping her on her back. Trying to get her to spurt into life.*

MIDWIFE. She's alive.

MARY. She?

MIDWIFE. Yes.

MARY. Another girl. She's not crying.

MIDWIFE. She's a weak little thing. Pale.

MARY. Breathing?

MIDWIFE. Just. I'm not sure she's got much of your spirit.

She hands her over to MARY.

MARY. Oh. She has. She has you'll see. Come on, little one.

The MIDWIFE *pinches the baby who begins to cry.*

ACT ONE 15

MIDWIFE. She'll need those lungs in the world. Best learn to use them.

MARY. Shhhhh. Shhhh. That's good. That's really good.

The MIDWIFE *starts to clean up.* MARY *looks at her daughter. Exhausted.*

Another girl.

MIDWIFE. You wanted a boy?

MARY. No. Expected maybe but not. Wanted exactly. Just.

MIDWIFE. Yes.

MARY. It's harder. Isn't it? With a girl. You love them so much. You love them so much and –

You know how the world will treat them.

I want to bring her up to know her principles and her mind and her power. And I want her to be happy, to be loved. And I fear so much that the world will force her to sacrifice one or the other.

So what should I do? Unfold her mind and make her sick of the world she is to inhabit? Leave her ignorant and half of what she could be?

MIDWIFE. Well. That's the question. The big one.

MARY. And what's the answer?

The MIDWIFE *shrugs.*

MIDWIFE. If I knew that, then, well, I might not be here with my hands up your chuff. But, I think you can't choose what they'll face, you just love them and you let them know it. And you fight –

You fight for it to be easier for them than it was for you, fight with everything you've got.

MARY. Yes. I'll try.

MIDWIFE. Oh and, maybe don't call this one Fanny?

MARY. What?

MIDWIFE. You know. If you want her to have a bit of an easier life.

MARY. Oh.

MIDWIFE. Just a thought.

MARY. Right. Yes.

> MARY *hums a little snatch of 'How'd You Grow a Girl' to her baby, a snatch of underscore floats by and starts to take us somewhere darker.*
>
> *The* MIDWIFE *is looking worried. She peers back under* MARY*'s legs. Fusses around.*

What's wrong?

MIDWIFE. You're not having any more pains?

MARY. No. No not that I can /

MIDWIFE. You should have fully delivered by now.

MARY. Fully?

MIDWIFE. The afterbirth. It's not coming.

MARY. Oh.

MIDWIFE. Sometimes if we wait.

MARY. What will happen?

MIDWIFE. It can rot. We should get the doctor.

MARY. I said no doctors.

MIDWIFE. Mary.

MARY. No doctors. It is your knowledge I trust. Women have been doing this for thousands of years.

MIDWIFE. Mr Godwin has said –

MARY. Mr Godwin, unless I have been deeply deceived, has limited personal expertise on the matter, never having done it himself.

MIDWIFE. If there were complications he said –

MARY. I don't want a doctor.

MIDWIFE. Mary.

MARY. No.

The MIDWIFE *nods at one of* THE HYENAS. *Suddenly a* DOCTOR *is at* MARY*'s bedside.* MARY *is incapacitated, legs apart.*

DOCTOR. Mrs Godwin /

MARY. Wollstonecraft-Godwin.

DOCTOR. Yes. Legs up please.

MARY. I don't want /

DOCTOR. Ahh yes I can see.

MARY. I said I don't want /

DOCTOR. Quiet yourself please. I can see the problem. Afterbirth not delivered. It shouldn't be too complicated.

MARY. What shouldn't be?

DOCTOR. Removal.

MARY. She said we could wait. Didn't you? We could wait a while.

MIDWIFE. I… Well if the doctor thinks.

MARY. What do you think?

DOCTOR. Risk of puerperal fever. Much simpler if I extract.

MARY. I don't want / you

DOCTOR. Don't worry yourself. I've done it many times. It's normal for women to be nervous of such things but you just concern yourself with your baby.

The DOCTOR *plunges his hands in.*

MARY. Ahhhhh. GOD.

DOCTOR. Nothing to make a fuss about.

MARY. Easy for you to say with a hand up my – Ahhhhh.

DOCTOR. Keep still, please.

> MARY *lies still. Alone. She is clearly sick now. Feverish. Pale. Sweaty. Eyes unfocused. She murmurs. Things have become really fragmented.*

MARY. Cold. I feel very cold. I.

> THE HYENAS *creep in. Prowl around her bedside. She turns her head, clocking them, confused.*
>
> *To* MARY *they have the faces of those in her life: the Midwife or Doctor, Marguerite, her sisters. Blurry, swimming in and out of focus.*
>
> *They loom large, flit around. She struggles to grasp onto them.*

HYENA. You've got a fever.

MARY. William? No. Marguerite, or who /

HYENA. The doctor introduced an infection. He didn't wash his hands.

MARY. Who, who are you?

HYENA. Ten days.

> *The music starts underneath the action.*
>
> *The clock changes. Now it is a countdown – ten days displayed.* MARY *starts, confused, but more awake.*

MARY. What?

HYENA. That's how long you've got.

MARY. What do you mean?

HYENA. Ten days. That's how long you live. From now. From the fever starting.

MARY. No, no, that can't be right. I've still got to, wait, you, you're, you're –

MARY *meets the eyes of one of* THE HYENAS *across the bed. She nods.*

But no, you're just a baby, you're there, you're –

THE HYENA *walks across to baby* MARY SHELLEY, *picks her up, and suddenly they are one.*

MARY S *and* MARY *look at each other, locked together.*

Here. Here all grown up.

MARY S. Ten days, Mum. That's how long we've got. That's how long you know me for.

MARY. No. No that can't be true, it / can't

MARY *scrambles out of bed. She and her daughter face each other.*

MARY S. It is, that's why we're here, all of us. So you can tell us –

MARY. What?

MARY S. Everything.

THE HYENAS *begin to sing.* MARY *and* MARY S *circle each other, locked together.*

Song: 'How'd You Grow a Girl'.

HYENAS.
How'd you grow a girl
In this world / in this world
How'd you grow a girl
How'd you grow a girl

How do you raise them
Protect them / save them
In an unfair world
In an unfair world

There's a thought in your brain
In a world that's insane
How to offer them a life
(Mother/daughter/slut/whore/TikTok trad-wife – ugh – no!)

**How'd you grow a girl
In this world / in this world
How'd you grow a girl**

**There's a thought in your head
I want her brave and fierce and well read
Have the world as her own
But it's not (she'll see that once she's grown)**

MARY. My baby. God. There's so much I want to tell you. Ask you.

MARY S. And I you.

MARY. You will never know me. Ten days. You won't remember me. You won't remember me at all.

MARY S. But I read. I read every word you ever wrote again and again and again. I want so much to know you. I try.

MARY. And you. What are you like? I will never know what you're like.

MARY S. No. No, but on my best days, I hope, I hope I'm like you.

MARY. There's so much I still need to do. For all of you. The world –

MARY S. Yes, yes but that's why we're here. You just have to tell us what to do.

They reach out to each other across the bed. Almost touching.

HYENAS.
**How'd you grow a girl
In this world / in this world
How'd you grow a girl**

**There's a battle in your soul
Do I tell her about a world that's out of control?
Where disparity exists
That's the patriarchy's wish**

**There's a cold hard fact
She'll be told how to act
And you prepare her for war
With her heart as her sword**

**How'd you grow a girl
In this world / in this world
How'd you grow a girl**

MARY. Ten days.

MARY S. Yes.

MARY. It's not enough.

MARY S. No. But it's all the time we have.

MARY. So we have to try.

MARY S nods. They spin. And fall –

Chapter One: Beverley, 1773

The stage is transformed into eighteenth century Beverley, the Wollstonecrafts' family home.

MARY, fourteen, sits scribbling outside a door. Night-time.

MARY W. Beverley. 1773.

The sound of a door and a man's heavy footsteps. He brandishes a whisky bottle at us.

EDWARD. Edward Wollstonecraft, father, patriarch, prick.

One of the HYENAS leans overs and blows out her candle.

A loud sound. EDWARD has tripped over MARY.

What the fuck –

MARY lights a lamp and stands up. EDWARD is on the floor, laid out. Confused.

Mary? What are you /

MARY. You need to sleep elsewhere tonight, Father.

EDWARD. Excuse me?

MARY. You can't go in there tonight.

EDWARD. I'll go where I damned well please.

MARY. Not tonight.

EDWARD. My own room? In my own house? Get out of my way, girl.

He goes to get up.

MARY. You've been drinking.

EDWARD. I won't answer to you.

MARY. I won't pick Mother off the floor again.

EDWARD. You'll do what I want. And thank me for it.

MARY. I won't.

EDWARD. Out of my way, Mary.

MARY. No.

EDWARD. I mean it.

MARY. So do I.

EDWARD. I am not in the mood for insolence.

MARY. And I not for violence but here we are.

EDWARD. You really are an impudent little slattern, aren't you?

He strikes MARY *across the face. She collapses downwards but doesn't step aside.*

OUT OF MY WAY.

MARY. NO.

Her mother, ELIZABETH, *appears behind her.*

ELIZABETH. Edward?

EDWARD *kicks* MARY *a couple of times.*

Edward, what's going on?

EDWARD. Your daughter thinks she's some sort of knight in shining armour.

ELIZABETH. I don't understand.

MARY. You think it does nothing to us? To hear Mother night after night? To hear her cries. You think we don't judge you? That we don't matter because we are nothing to you? Well we do. Judge you. I do. And you should be ashamed. I know what is right and wrong because I feel it – here. No matter if the world says you can do as you please. I feel it. Deep here I feel it is wrong and I will not be silent and watch.

I will not.

ELIZABETH. She doesn't mean it. Edward. She doesn't.

MARY. I do.

He lurches towards MARY, *she flinches. He laughs.*

EDWARD. Not so bold after all. Well stay there all night if you want, I don't care.

EDWARD *turns to go. Thinks better of it.*

Oh and since you've kindly waited up for me, I'll share some news. We're leaving in the morning. For London. I've got a very good lead on some business.

ELIZABETH. London?

MARY. But, but I can't. My school. My friends. I won't go. I won't do it.

EDWARD. Don't then. Stay here for all I care. Dirty the gutter.

MARY. I hate you.

ELIZABETH. What a spiteful thing to say. I'm ashamed of you Mary. Apologise.

MARY. No.

EDWARD. There's a carriage coming at midday. Make sure the children's things are packed.

MARY. I hate you. I hate you. I hate you.

For a second it looks like he will hit her again, but instead he sneers.

EDWARD. And control this bitch, Elizabeth. I mean it.

He strides out the room.

ELIZABETH. You shouldn't have provoked him, Mary.

MARY. I would not have him do it again. I couldn't. For your sake.

ELIZABETH. For my sake? Who asked you to speak for me?

MARY. I thought you would –

ELIZABETH. What? Thank you? Thank you for provoking him and humiliating me in the middle of the night? Go to bed, Mary.

She leaves. MARY *is left alone.*

MARY. I won't go. They can't make me. They – But they would leave me here. All alone.

Maybe it is me. Maybe I am the only one in the world that feels like this. A fire burning in the pit of my stomach. It says this is wrong. They are wrong.

But what if I am wrong? Made wrong? Just as everyone seems to think.

The music begins.

What then?

MARY *begins to sing.*

Song: 'Run Wild'.

Be a good girl – they ask me
Be a good girl they say
Don't you – react badly
Just do whatever they say
You know it's got to be their way
The world's just that way
It's easier if it's their way anyway

As she sings the family come in and pack their things.
ELIZABETH *throws a suitcase at* MARY.

ELIZABETH. Pack.

Reluctantly MARY *gets up. She clutches her suitcase, downtrodden still. The* HYENAS *join her in singing.*

MARY/THE HYENAS.
Take a step back – in the shadows
Don't speak in public at all
Don't you – try and do the right thing
You just do as you're told
You know it's got to be his way
It's a man's job to shine
We just sit at on the side

Oh no
Oh no
Oh no
Oh no

Be pretty and lovely and pleasing
Not too much – they'll think you're teasing
Have things to say so amusing
Not too much – they'll find it confusing

It's a man's job to shine (It's a man's job to shine)
It's a man's job to shine (It's a man's job to shine)
Oh no
Oh no

The family and MARY *cram into a carriage, suitcases piled high, they set off for London.*

I try – yeah I try
To shrink myself down
Do as they ask
Wear a feminine mask
But I just want to run wild
Breathe big air in the big fields
And let the big thoughts grow
Have the courage to tell them
Tell them all what I already know

MARY *breaks free of the carriage, clawing her way out. She reaches* MARY S *and together they sing. Running. Jumping over suitcases. Free.*

That I – just wanna run wild
I just wanna run wild
I wanna run willllldddded

MARY (*to* MARY S). Never let anyone make you believe the world is too small for you. Promise me. Never.

MARY/THE HYENAS.
I can think and hope and reason
Yeah I know what is right and is wrong
I just need a little bit of freedom
Whatever I do it seems wrong
Whatever I am it feels wrong
Whatever I do it seems wrong
Whatever I am it feels wrong
Feels wrong
Feels wrong
Feels wrong

MARY S. Do you go?

MARY. Of course I go.

MARY S. And what happens?

MARY. Well for a while I am very lonely.

MARY S. And then?

MARY. And then –

Chapter Two: London, 1774

MARY *sits on her suitcase. Her hair greasy. Her clothes unkempt. She is depressed. She clutches a book. John Locke.*

MARY. London, 1774.

She opens her book and reads it with a fervour.

A knock on the door. She ignores it.

Another. She does not even look up.

Another.

The knocker looks at us and speaks.

ELIZA. Eliza Wollstonecraft, sister of Mary. Largely ignored.

She knocks again.

Like now.

EVERINA *pops up*.

EVERINA. And me. Everina Wollstonecraft. I'm the youngest. Well, the youngest girl anyhow.

ELIZA *goes back to knocking*. MARY *goes back to ignoring her.*

ELIZA. Mary.

Mary, we have company.

Mary.

Mary, open the door.

They've come to visit you especially.

Mary.

MARY *looks up*.

MARY. Who is it?

ELIZA. Miss Blood.

MARY rushes to the door. Smooths her hair. Opens it. Sees her sisters. Is disappointed.

MARY. Where is she?

ELIZA. Downstairs.

MARY falters, goes back for her book.

Are you coming? You've not left this room in weeks.

MARY. I'm reading.

EVERINA. Mother is furious. You should hear what she is saying about you in the kitchen. Lazy, ignorant, rude, neglectful /

ELIZA. Everina.

EVERINA. She says she wishes she'd never had you.

MARY. I thought this is what she wanted: be quiet, stay out the way, don't cause trouble. But no, still it seems better that I shouldn't exist.

ELIZA. Mary. We are all adjusting. Life here is different.

MARY. Not different enough.

FANNY appears in the doorway. Bathed in glowing light, she looks almost angelic. Maybe there is sound. Think fairy godmother, this is MARY*'s memory, not real.*

FANNY. Fanny Blood. The love of her life, ready to join the sisterhood.

ELIZA. Yes. Fanny Blood. As you might have already clocked, there are several fannies in this story.

FANNY. That's feminism.

MARY *is transfixed.*

I'm sorry to intrude, I could always come back if now's not a / good time –

MARY. No. No. I want to meet you. Very much. I was just, not dressed for, I wasn't expecting –

She's embarrassed. FANNY *swiftly makes her at ease.*

FANNY. You are reading?

MARY. Locke. John Locke.

FANNY. 'Life, liberty and property.'

MARY. You know it! Did you like it?

FANNY. Yes. I think so. I must confess I am not as adept at philosophy as I would like. I find some of it, difficult.

EVERINA. Mary lives for difficult. The boringer the better.

ELIZA. Everina.

EVERINA. What? She does.

MARY. He writes things I've felt but I haven't the language for. He writes that a man should have no more power over his wife than she over him. Did you know that? We are all born free and equal. All of us.

EVERINA. Tell that to Mother when she's making us do the beds and not Ned.

MARY. I have tried.

FANNY. I can see you feel what he is writing in your heart.

MARY. He writes things that make me feel less alone. Can you understand that?

FANNY. Yes. Yes I can.

She reaches out and touches her hand for a second. The intimacy thrills MARY. *She is being recognised.*

MARY. I heard that you paint?

FANNY. Yes.

MARY. And sell it?

FANNY. Sometimes.

MARY. And people pay you. You earn your own money. Support your family. Depend on no one.

FANNY. We all depend on someone or we would be very lonely.

MARY. I plan to depend on no one.

FANNY. Really?

MARY. Well I thought so, until just now.

ELIZA. We heard you were to be married, Miss Blood. Are there many suitors round here?

EVERINA. Eliza is desperate to get married.

ELIZA. Everina.

EVERINA. What? It's true.

FANNY. It is true I am to be married. I can't say I know many suitors however. Mr Skeys, my fiancé, lives in Portugal. I am waiting until he has enough money to send for me.

ELIZA. Oh. I see.

MARY. And you do not worry for your independence?

FANNY. A little.

EVERINA. None of us can be *independent*, Mary, we're girls, stupid.

MARY. Who told you that?

EVERINA. Ned.

MARY. Well, you don't have to believe him. I'll never marry. And you shouldn't either if you don't want to.

ELIZA. Mary.

EVERINA. Mary is very obstinate my father says. Like a mule.

ELIZA. Did you hear that in the kitchen too?

EVERINA. Yes.

MARY. Being tied to a tyrant is bad enough as a daughter or sister, I will not bear it as a wife.

ELIZA. I would like to be married. To be loved and cared for. Have a family. Have a life.

MARY. A life is exactly what you might sacrifice.

ELIZA. We're allowed to have different dreams you know, Mary.

MARY. Not in this world we're not.

ELIZA. What else are we meant to do? We cannot work, we cannot inherit. Living on debt and promises forever. I won't do it. I can't think of anything worse.

MARY. But, your liberty /

FANNY. Is all we have to trade.

MARY. Well, the price is too much. Surely now that I've found you I cannot let you just be whisked away.

FANNY. No?

MARY. No. You know I have been very low. I have been very alone, but suddenly I feel that maybe I have found –

FANNY. A friend.

Hope.

MARY *and* FANNY *really look at each other.*

They begin to sing to each other.

Song: 'Find Your Tribe'.

MARY/FANNY.
There's a moment when I see you
And everything just stops
For the first time
In a long time
I know you feel my heart
Deep within my soul
I feel you
You feel me
And it heals me
It heals me

When you're lonely
And hopeless
And inches from despair
When the world seems cold and heartless
And no one seems to care

Find your tribe
Find your women
Find the girls who've got your back
Find the ones who never leave you
And even save you from yourself
No romance
No fathers
No hunks who let you dowwwwwwn
If you're lucky
Find your tribe and go wiiiiiiild

MARY. I will take care of you. All of you. I promise. I will find a way if it kills me. Then you don't need to marry. Then we can be free.

MARY/FANNY.
See that life, I don't accept it
It seems a bit extreme
And the more of us
That think this way
We can keep our liberty
Deep within my soul
I feel you
You feel me
And it heals me
It heals me

When you're lonely
And hopeless
And inches from despair
When the world seems cold and heartless
Is there anyone out there?

Find your tribe
Find your women
Find the girls who've got your back
Find the ones who never leave you
And even save you from yourself
No romance
No fathers
No hunks who let you dowwwwwwn

**If you're lucky
Find your tribe and go wiiiiiiild
If you're lucky
Find your tribe and go wiiiiiiild**

**Yeah yeah
Yeeeaaaahhh
Yeaaaahhh
Alright!**

FANNY. I admire your spirit.

MARY. You don't believe me I can see, but you should know I have never yet resolved to do something and not accomplished it.

FANNY. I believe you. I have no doubt in you. I would not dare.

They hug.

FANNY, ELIZA *and* EVERINA *leave. A turning, the clock ticks over to nine days.*

A bed is wheeled in, ELIZABETH *lies in it.* MARY *blanches, swallows.*

MARY S. Are you okay?

MARY. Yes. Yes, just. I hoped I'd never have to do this again.

MARY S. It's never easy, is it, saying goodbye.

MARY *looks at her, recognises that's what she's having to do too.*

MARY. No. No it's not.

She reluctantly marches up to the bed and tucks her mother in.

London 1781.

Chapter Three: London, 1781

ELIZABETH *is dying*. MARY *is trying to make her eat*.

MARY. Mother, you must try and eat something.

—

Please. I think if you tried it you would like it.

—

Do you want to get better? I know you haven't been happy for a long time. And now I can't help feeling you just don't want to.

ELIZABETH. Edward. Edward.

MARY. No it's Mary.

ELIZABETH. Edward.

MARY. Mary. It's Mary.

ELIZABETH. Oh.

She turns away, determinedly ignoring the food.

MARY. You don't want to be better because then you would have to admit he has never once come when you called him, in all these years. You have put up with it all for nothing and now he won't even come when you are dying.

ELIZABETH. Ned.

MARY. Or him. Busy at court he says, though none of us believe it.

ELIZABETH. Ned.

MARY. Not too busy to spend every coin the family name puts in his pocket and wait for the rest once you're gone. But too busy, too busy to come.

ELIZABETH. Mary. I need to see Ned. Please.

MARY. He's not coming.

ELIZABETH. It would give me such comfort to see him. Don't keep him from me. You always were a jealous girl. Never content, always wanting attention. But don't keep him from me now. My darling baby boy. Don't keep him from me out of spite.

MARY. Spite?

—

Eliza is to be married. I'm sure she's told you. A friend of Ned's and Mr Skeys'. They seem to think he's a very good prospect. Maybe he is. But, we don't really know him.

Maybe you could talk to her? She won't listen to me. She thinks I'm spoiling her dreams.

MARY *waits but* ELIZABETH *doesn't answer.*

What did you hope for us? When we were first born. Me, Eliza and Everina?

Please?

I know you have borne many things. I know you couldn't bring yourself to love us. Me.

I know you couldn't bring yourself to love me.

But, when we were first pulled from you, all of us. When you held us for the first time. What life did you hope we might have? How did you think it might be different to yours?

She waits.

ELIZABETH. Ned.

MARY. Tell me, please. Because I am trying so hard. I am trying so hard to hope, to believe it might be different. But I am struggling to see how we make it so.

ELIZABETH. Ned.

MARY. Did you ever hope? For the three of us. Did you waste any hopes at all?

ELIZABETH. If Ned /

MARY. He's not coming. He's not interested.

MARY takes the uneaten soup and turns away, collecting herself.

ELIZABETH. I do not want you. You are not who I want.

MARY. Can you not be angry with them, Mother? For me. Can you not be angry with how they have left us? Can you not curse them? Please. Because this, this I cannot bear.

ELIZABETH. He will be here soon.

MARY. Curse them.

ELIZABETH. Such a successful busy boy.

MARY. I want to hear it. I want to hear your rage.

ELIZABETH grasps her hand, for a second MARY hopes then she speaks.

ELIZABETH. A little patience and all will be over.

She dies. MARY looks at her, she can't believe it.

THE HYENAS *circle her and begin to sing.*

Song: 'A Little Patience'.

THE HYENAS.
A little patience
Things will get better
A little patience
Don't push us too far
We're on the road to
Some kind of progress
A little patience

Ask nicely
Smile sweetly
Your life is
A misery

In the background we see ELIZA come in her wedding dress, MEREDITH in a suit beside her. They marry.

Another life wasted
Another hope lost
I open my eyes
And we're back to the start
A woman betrayed
By the beat of her heart

A little patience
A little
FUCCCCCCKKKK
FUCCCCKKKK
FUUUUUUUUUUUUUUUUUUUUCCCCCK

MARY. Fuck that.

And MARY *is on her feet. Putting on her coat, running out the door.*

MARY S. What do we do now?

MARY. Anything. Anything to stop it happening again.

A swirl and she is gone.

Chapter Four: Hackney, 1783

Arrives at ELIZA, *panting she announces –*

MARY. Hackney, 1783.

She grabs ELIZA *and beckons to* MARY S *to help.*

MARY S. What are we doing?

MARY. We're staging a rescue.

ELIZA *starts to shed her wedding items, fleeing with the three women. There is an element of glee.*

MEREDITH. What's going on? Excuse me. That's my wife you're holding.

MARY S. Sorry but your wife is getting the fuck out of here.

As they flee, MARY *begins to sing, joined by the rest of* THE HYENAS. *They leave a trail of wedding paraphernalia behind them. For a bit it feels exciting and intoxicating.*

MARY. It's time to effect a revolution in female manners.

The song begins. MARY *sweeps* ELIZA *away.*

Song: 'Utopian Dreams'.

ELIZA. Where are we going?

MARY. I don't know. Anywhere! Anywhere better.

(*Singing.*)

I've always said
We must act and not talk
If we wanna save her
If we want to save ourselves

We must fight
For a different future
But where are we going?
And will the dream collide?

We're going to start a school. All of us. Living together. Teaching together. Think of it.

I think about the planes of equality
I think about a house that's just ours
I think if money were no object
I think I'd reach for freedom amongst the stars

They may only be
Utopian dreams
But I gotta feelin'
They're not goin' anywhere
Want you to see
Utopian dreams
House with a ceiling
In Newington Green

EVERINA. Eliza wanted to be married, Mary.

ELIZA. I couldn't stay, Everina. It was, he was, horror.

> **I don't ask for much**
> **Just a place where we know**
> **If we wanna break out**
> **If we want to have ideas**
>
> **A place for us all**
> **With the freedom to live**
> **The power of knowledge**
> **And the courage to play**

MARY. This is it. This is how I take care of all of you. This is how we escape.

> **I think of us united in the fight now**
> **I think about time the world is yours**
> **I think about the girls of the future**
> **I think about them tearing down the walls**
>
> **They may only be**
> **Utopian dreams**
> **But I gotta feelin'**
> **They're not goin' anywhere**
> **Want you to see**
> **Utopian dreams**
> **House with a ceiling**
> **In Newington Green**
> **World with a meanin'**
> **In Newington Green**
> **More than a feelin'**
> **In Newington Green**

MARY *grabs the others and starts to build a classroom. Dragging them along with her, into the future.*

All of us. Free. Independent. Teaching girls to cultivate their minds and bodies, to be able to speak for themselves, articulate themselves on their own terms. A new world. Imagine.

The song finishes. The atmosphere changes, reality creeping in.

MARY S. It sounds amazing.

MARY. Yes.

MARY S. But –

MARY. No buts.

MARY S. Mary.

MARY. No.

MARY S. But?

MARY. But, there's always a point with dreams where reality sets in. And teaching is hard. And the winter is freezing. And, Eliza is free but. But she has to leave her baby behind. And, without her mother, she dies. That winter, Eliza's baby dies.

But we can't stop to feel it. Because it's too sad.

And because we are too busy, too busy changing things.

The clock changes to eight days.

School bell. MARY *turns away and starts to chalk lessons on the chalkboard*

Newington Green 1784.

Chapter Five: Newington Green, 1784

MARY *teaching.*

MARY. So. *The Tempest,* what do we think?

PUPIL. Shakespeare's writing is sublime, he is a genius.

MARY. No.

PUPIL. No?

MARY. I mean it may be. But why are you saying that?

PUPIL. I, I don't understand.

MARY. I want you to think. Don't parrot ideas back at me but think for yourselves. What do you, you, think?

PUPIL. I... I.

MARY. Why is he sublime and a genius?

PUPIL. It says so in this book.

MARY. And why should we trust that book?

PUPIL. Because you gave it to us.

MARY. But what do I know?

PUPIL. Miss?

MARY. I want your thoughts. Not mine. Not theirs. Know others' opinions, yes. Respect them, if they deserve it. But question them. Build on them. If you need to, disagree.

PUPIL. Question Shakespeare?

MARY. Write it down. Write me an answer. What do you think of this play? Think honestly, rigorously, use your knowledge, but above all think for yourselves. Bring it to me tomorrow.

PUPIL. Yes, Miss Wollstonecraft.

MARY. Now, off you go. Painting with Miss Blood next.

EVERINA *comes in*.

EVERINA. Are you encouraging them to insurrection? I can hardly keep them in line as it is.

MARY. Just to think, Everina.

EVERINA. I don't want them to think, I want them to behave.

MARY. Can you check they get to Fanny?

EVERINA. They don't respect me you know.

MARY. Well, do you respect them? Maybe if you sulked less they would enjoy your lessons.

EVERINA. Eliza is crying again.

MARY. Again?

EVERINA. She says she cannot teach this afternoon.

MARY. I see.

EVERINA. She is grieving, Mary.

MARY. I know. You will have to take them, me and Fanny are going out.

EVERINA. Out?

MARY. Dr Price's sermon. He is talking about America, the new treaty, it is such a success, Everina, for freedom, for all of us. Revolution is possible.

EVERINA. Hooray. I won't bother making up the schoolroom fires then, I'll revolt instead.

MARY. Everina.

EVERINA. Well, I can't help it, Mary. You are always out. We are always here. Trying to get grubby children to wash their faces, and not let their parents sneak away without paying their fees.

MARY. You are welcome to come, you and Eliza, but I thought you didn't like these visits.

EVERINA. I don't. But I would like to be asked.

EVERINA turns to go.

MARY. Everina?

EVERINA. Yes?

MARY. We are all here together. Working, independent, free /

EVERINA. I don't feel very free.

MARY. We've worked so hard to make this happen, Everina, protect it. Why not even try to enjoy it?

EVERINA. Sometimes you are quite unbearable.

She leaves. MARY *calls.*

MARY. Only sometimes?

MARY puts on her coat and spins.

Suddenly we are in Newington Green Unitarian Church. MARY *and* FANNY *sit on the benches*

DR PRICE *appears and introduces himself.*

DR PRICE. Dr Price. Famous insurrectionary preacher. Philosopher. Beard-sporter. Rebellion-inciter.

He mounts the pulpit and launches full throttle into his sermon.

Why are the nations of the world so patient under despotism? Why do they crouch to tyrants, and submit to be treated as if they were a herd of cattle? Enlighten them and you will elevate them. Shew them they are men, and they will act like men.

Behold kingdoms, admonished by you, starting from sleep, breaking their fetters, and claiming justice from their oppressors! Behold!

He finishes. MARY *and* FANNY *are on their feet applauding.*

FANNY *is struggling to breathe a little in the excitement. She coughs.*

MARY. I find it so hopeful. To believe. The world is getting better, all around us Europe is stirring. Ideas, new ways of living, possibilities, and we are a part of it, Fanny. We are.

More coughing.

FANNY. I did like it, but I do wish he would speak a little louder.

MARY. Fanny.

FANNY. Well, sometimes it all goes into his beard, and I am left not enlightened at all.

They laugh. It descends into a long coughing fit.

MARY. Fanny? Are you?

FANNY. I'm fine. Quite well. Don't fuss.

MARY. We should sit.

FANNY. I am fine.

MARY makes them sit down to rest for a minute.

MARY. This cold isn't doing any good. Have you got your coat fully buttoned?

FANNY. Yes.

MARY. I would buy you a new one if we had the money.

FANNY. Don't fuss, Mary.

MARY. Mr Skeys would.

FANNY. In Portugal I wouldn't need one.

MARY. Have you thought any more about his / offer

FANNY. I am happy here.

MARY. Your chest, it is worse. If I am being selfish /

FANNY. You're not.

MARY. You did love him?

FANNY. A bit. Liked anyway. But years it's been now. I can hardly remember him. And you, you I very much remember.

MARY. Yes. And I you.

FANNY. He humiliated me, Mary. He made me wait so long and then to write to me now and just expect me to drop everything and come, like I, like –

She coughs so much she can't continue.

MARY. Yes. Yes I know, I just want you to be well.

They are interrupted by DR PRICE *and* MR JOHNSON, *who have caught up with them from church.*

DR PRICE. Miss Wollstonecraft.

MARY. Dr Price.

DR PRICE. I hope you enjoyed the sermon.

MARY. We did. 'Enlighten them and you will elevate them.' I thought I might put that on my school literature. And then I thought it would be too expensive, but the sentiment rings true.

DR PRICE. Miss Wollstonecraft and Miss Blood run a school. Quite brilliant. Teach young women with proper ideals in the true spirit of radicalism.

MARY. Well. In the spirit of cultivating brains and minds. And in the spirit of me and my sisters being able to afford bread.

DR PRICE. This is Mr Johnson.

JOHNSON. Joseph Johnson. Patron, publisher, purveyor of radical thoughts and dissenting minds.

DR PRICE. And one of our supper club regulars, although I don't think your paths have yet crossed.

MARY. No. I'm sorry to say not.

JOHNSON. What is it you teach in your school, Miss Wollstonecraft?

MARY. We teach girls to use reason. To value their own minds and their own opinions. I believe each student is an individual and must be treated as such.

JOHNSON. That is quite unusual.

MARY. So I understand.

JOHNSON. It is quite in fashion at the minute, the issue of female education. If you might consider a pamphlet I could publish.

MARY. I would hope the issue of female education was more than a fashion.

JOHNSON. I hope so too, but perhaps you could help to persuade others.

FANNY *stifles a cough.*

MARY. We must get you home. The cold is not good for my friend's chest.

FANNY. No need to fuss.

FANNY gets up but is overcome with coughing.

JOHNSON. Are you well, Miss Blood?

FANNY. Oh quite –

She cannot finish because of her cough.

– fine.

JOHNSON. Are you sure?

FANNY. Quite, thank you. Just a little –

Again she can't get her words out.

Just.

She bends double.

Mary.

MARY *runs to help her.*

I think I must –

FANNY *collapses. Spits blood onto the floor.*

DR PRICE. Could, is there a doctor? Could someone fetch?

FANNY. I just need. To rest.

JOHNSON. Is your friend?

MARY. Tuberculosis.

DR PRICE. Oh.

FANNY *stops coughing but folds in on herself. Head on the floor.*

JOHNSON. She needs to be careful in this cold. We should get a doctor.

DR PRICE. Yes. I will go.

He leaves to fetch a DOCTOR.

JOHNSON. Have they advised, I mean, it seems advanced?

MARY. It is worse. Much worse than I have allowed myself to believe.

JOHNSON. Can anything be done?

MARY *looks at* FANNY, *she resolves*.

MARY. She must go abroad. They said maybe a warmer climate. She must go to Portugal.

Very quietly and weakly FANNY *objects*.

FANNY. Mary.

MARY. To be married. Her fiancé lives there.

FANNY. Mary

JOHNSON. Oh, well that seems very fortunate.

MARY. Does it?

Chapter Six: Portugal, 1785

A church bell tolls.

MARY. Portugal. 1785.

FANNY *rises up, looks at* MARY *one last time and walks off.*

No.

MARY *struggles to go after her.* THE HYENAS *hold her back. They start to dress her in black.*

Maybe as FANNY *disappears we hear an echo of 'A Little Patience', sung hauntingly.*

No. No please.

Fanny's tombstone rises through the stage in front of MARY.

No. This was meant to save you. Marrying him was meant to save you. That was the whole point. This was meant to make you better.

Please don't go. Please don't leave me. What do I have to go back home for now?

Fanny. Without you. What do I have without you?

She sinks to her knees. Fanny's grave sinks.

ELIZA *and* EVERINA *appear either side of* MARY.

EVERINA. What do we do now?

MARY. I don't know.

EVERINA. There are no pupils left. They're all gone. Without you and Fanny their parents didn't want them to stay.

MARY. You could have got more.

ELIZA. We tried.

MARY. I see.

EVERINA. We owe on rent. They won't let us stay much longer.

MARY. Yes.

EVERINA. We told you we couldn't do it on our own.

MARY. It was my fault she was there. Mine. I had to go.

EVERINA. You told us you'd look after us. You promised us we could have a life all of us together.

MARY. I know.

EVERINA. Eliza left her husband, her baby /

MARY. I KNOW. Do you think I don't know? I know and the weight of it is drowning me.

ELIZA. Mary.

MARY. You're right. It didn't work. None of it worked. And now, what you do now, I'm sorry but that's not my responsibility. You are not my responsibility. Any more. You can't be any more.

ELIZA. Mary.

MARY. I can't carry you on my own. I'm too tired. I'm exhausted. Why can you not, for once, take care of yourselves? WHY?

—

ELIZA. We don't know how, Mary. We're not like you.

—

MARY. That's probably a good thing. In the end. That's probably better. Who would want to be like me?

ELIZA. Mary.

MARY. It's true.

—

ELIZA. What will you do? Now?

Slowly MARY *brings out a letter.*

MARY. I've been offered a governess position in Ireland.

EVERINA. Ireland? It's so far away.

MARY. There isn't another option. I'll try to send money, once I'm there.

A second. Suddenly they all hug.

I'm sorry. I'm sorry I couldn't take care of you. You were right, it was just a dream after all.

They let go, hand her suitcase, and walk away. MARY *stands small and defeated.*

The clock ticks over: seven days.

Suddenly a trumpet plays.

Ireland. 1786.

Chapter Seven: Ireland, 1786

A grand hall. LADY KINGSBOROUGH *sweeps in, grandly dressed and, following her, a pack of pampered pooches.*

She stands and coquettes, as if addressing a crowd.

LADY KINGSBOROUGH. Oh welcome to our humble hall,
We own half of Ireland, what a bore!
We're Aristocrats – English, of course, Lord and Lady Kingsborough.

An extra little flourish, as if conducting an orchestra. She sweeps down upon MARY.

MARY. Mary, Mary Wollstonecraft.

LADY KINGSBOROUGH. Oh, the new governess.

MARY. Yes.

LADY KINGSBOROUGH. Enchanting. Enchanted to meet you.
Now I'm sure you'll find us charming.
Please don't find our grandeur too alarming
If you play your cards right, we might even extend an invitation,
Of an evening.

She examines MARY *as if she's a pig brought to market.*

You have different clothes, of course?

MARY. Er. Not really.

LADY KINGSBOROUGH. Oh. How dreadful.

She gathers herself. Pokes and prods MARY *a bit, whips her into shape.*

Still, perhaps with a witty remark,
Flutter your eyelashes, you'll capture our hearts.
We're all lords and ladies, the crème de la crème,

(You are, of course, inferior.)

But with a little powder, we might polish you into a gem.
There's always hope.

With a wave of her hand she dismisses her and starts to leave.

Now I've my coiffeur to see to, my babies to bathe,
The servants to reprimand and make to behave.
It's not easy being this grand and important,
But I'm sure you'll get used to us, just curtsy when talking.

MARY *awkwardly curtsies.*

MARY. Er, and after they are bathed you will send them to the schoolroom.

LADY KINGSBOROUGH. Pardon?

MARY. Will you send them to the schoolroom? I find children / take to

LADY KINGSBOROUGH. Oh the children. Will I send the children?

MARY. Well, yes.

LADY KINGSBOROUGH. I am not bathing the children. Oh. No, how extraordinary.

She picks up a dog and begins cooing and baby-talking it.

These are my babies, my darling little cutey-wootey girls,
my pwerfect pooches, darling darlings,
My sweetie-weetie gorgeous little furballs.

MARY. And the children?

LADY KINGSBOROUGH. Who cares.

A mob of screaming CHILDREN *rip through the hall, shouting and chasing and throwing things.*

Oh, there they are.

MARY. Yes.

The CHILDREN *rip back the other way.*

One of them stops and looks at us.

MARGARET. Margaret Kingsborough. Young lady, terror, tearaway, terroriser of governesses. One of many, but the only one you're going to care about.

She spits on the floor. They all run away. MARY *is left covered in some of the things they have thrown. Maybe a banana peel.*

LADY KINGSBOROUGH. Well. You've been introduced. Goodnight, Miss Wollstonecraft.

LADY KINGSBOROUGH *and her dogs saunter off, perhaps to another little trumpet.*

MARY *peels the banana off her face, above her* MARGARET *giggles.*

LADY KINGSBOROUGH *shouts back.*

And good luck.

Chapter Eight

MARY *sits down at her desk, reading some papers.* MARGARET *wriggles at her desk before her, itching to get up and destroy something.*

MARGARET. When is it time for our walk?

MARY. After lunch.

MARGARET. We never took walks before you got here.

MARY. Exercise is good vigour for the mind as well as the body.

MARGARET. Mother says I could do with altogether less vigour.

MARY. I can imagine she might say that.

MARGARET. I do try, but it is hard to be dull. I don't see why making yourself dull is what girls have to do.

MARY. I am not the person to ask, Margaret.

MARGARET. Sit still, Margaret. Smile, Margaret. Move less, Margaret. Don't ask so many questions. Don't spit /

MARY. That one I agree with /

MARGARET. Don't yawn. Don't laugh too loudly. Do NOT disagree or tell someone they're wrong, or get excited or run or climb or do anything that's worth doing at all. Just be a little mouse. I don't know why people want to marry little mice, they're very boring.

MARY. It is true, people often admire a woman if she is less herself, smaller. But I'm afraid I can't tell you how to achieve it because I have never been able to do it myself.

—

MARGARET. You are not at all like our other governesses.

MARY. No?

MARGARET. No. We had all quite determined to dislike you, normally it is not hard to dislike governesses but –

MARY. But?

MARGARET. But you are quite different.

MARY. Finish your exercises please, Margaret.

—

MARGARET. Why do you cry? At night?

MARY. Why would you ask that?

MARGARET. Your face is red and puffy often. In the mornings.

MARY. Right.

MARGARET. And, you seem sad.

MARY. Sorry?

MARGARET. You seem sad. Quite a lot of the time when I look at you. Your eyes are sad.

This has MARY *taken aback. No one has been so perceptive about her for a long time.*

MARY. Well. I suppose I am a little homesick. I miss my sisters, just as you would if you were thrust upon the world without them. They drive me mad as soon as I am with them but, here – And. I miss a dear friend who died. Who died recently and who was very important to me.

MARGARET. How did she die?

MARY. She was not very strong. And she had a baby.

MARGARET. Why did she have a baby if she wasn't very well?

MARY. She. Sometimes there is not a lot of choice in the matter.

MARGARET. Mother says I will have to have babies soon.

MARY. I am sure you need not worry about that yet.

MARGARET. She has already arranged my match. Her wedding was at sixteen, you see, so she says I don't have long. Father said I need to breed some more aristocrats for this godforsaken isle.

MARY. I'm sure the people of Ireland will be overjoyed at that.

MARGARET. Yes, he said so.

MARY. And what do you want, Margaret?

MARGARET. I don't know.

MARY. Do you want to be married? Or to work? To learn? What?

MARGARET. I haven't thought about it.

MARY. That is no excuse.

MARGARET is a bit taken aback. She thinks for a moment and then darts to pull out a book. It's an encyclopaedia about anatomy and dissection.

MARGARET. I found this in the library. It's got bodies, and people cut up, innards all spilling out, a kidney, look!

She turns to the goriest page hoping to shock.

ACT ONE, CHAPTER EIGHT 55

MARY. Anatomy. It's an emerging area of science I am told. Very interesting.

MARGARET. Do you think I could do something like that?

MARY. I don't know, Margaret. You could try. If you applied yourself.

MARGARET. I won't be able to apply myself with a husband, will I? I bet they get in the way.

MARY. A young woman of your potential needs to see the world. See it and make up your own mind.

MARGARET. Do I have potential?

MARY. Yes.

—

MARGARET. You've done a lot of things haven't you?

MARY. I am not sure, Margaret.

MARGARET. You have. You've been abroad, and you have a tragic friend who died, and your school, and you mention all these thinkers you've met, people who've written things. I want a life like that. I want not to get stuck. Being small in dressing rooms and drinking tea in drawing rooms. How do I do that?

MARY. I, I don't know. Sometimes I'm scared of getting stuck too.

MARGARET. I think you should write it all down. All those things you've done. So, we can work it out.

MARY looks at MARGARET, a bit of her old fire is coming into her belly.

MARY. Maybe. Maybe I shall try. If you resolve to try as well?

MARGARET. Deal.

MARY and MARGARET smile at each other and begin writing.

Chapter Nine

LADY KINGSBOROUGH *comes on and starts snatching the writing and pushing* MARY *out the door. She is beside herself.*

LADY KINGSBOROUGH. Out out out! There's a radical in the house.

MARY. What? What is happening?

LADY KINGSBOROUGH. Out out out! My child is refusing a spouse.

MARY. Lady Kingsborough, what's the /

LADY KINGSBOROUGH. OUT OUT OUT! Her mind has been poisoned! Her honour has been compromised!

MARY. I think this is a misunderstanding.

LADY KINGSBOROUGH. She's having her own ideas, she thinks she gets to decide! Horror of horrors! Shock of shocks! She says she won't be married.

MARY. I have never poisoned her mind, only encouraged her to think for herself.

LADY KINGSBOROUGH. OUT OUT OUT! So you admit it? Hmmmm! You're a nasty layabout. You've encouraged this defiance! You've nourished disrespect! You've tricked us all, you low-down... *whore*!

MARY. Excuse me?!

LADY KINGSBOROUGH. And now, now, NOW, your ideas have ruined my child.

MARY. This is totally unfair. I have only ever cherished Margaret's mind and tried to grow her soul.

LADY KINGSBOROUGH. Her mind?! Her mind! A girl of great breeding needs to look charming. Needs to coquette, fake interest in farming. Pop out babies, be shown off at parties. The last thing she needs is a mind!

MARY. Well, I'm afraid I disagree.

LADY KINGSBOROUGH. Disagree, disagree! As if you are paid to disagree. She is a Kingsborough!

MARY. She's a one-off.

LADY KINGSBOROUGH. She's an aristocrat!

MARY. She's a genius.

LADY KINGSBOROUGH. She's a disobedient little toe rag!

MARY. She's the future.

LADY KINGSBOROUGH. *SHE'S A GIRLLLLLLL.*

MARY. Exactly! I am sorry for you actually. Because she is a girl with a huge heart and mind and brave soul and you cannot see it. You will never see why you should be proud of her. And that is your loss.

LADY KINGSBOROUGH *is so overcome that she blows a raspberry at* MARY.

LADY KINGSBOROUGH. *GETTTTTT OUT.*

One final push and she exits with her dogs. MARY *sits down on her suitcases suddenly exhausted.*

MARY. Oh. God. What now?

MARGARET *sneaks up and throws her arms around her.*

MARGARET. Mary, I am so sorry.

MARY. No, it is not your fault, it's mine. I could not keep my mouth shut, as usual.

MARGARET. What are you going to do?

MARY. I, I really do not know.

MARGARET. You have changed my life forever. And you can do that for everyone. You can. You just need to show them what you've got to say.

She gives her the papers. MARY *looks at them.*

MARY S *who has been watching, picks up the suitcase and hands it to her.*

MARY S. She's right you know.

MARY *looks at both of them.*

MARY. Thank you.

MARY *makes her way back to London.*

As she goes THE HYENAS *mirror her. Singing her thoughts and backing her up like a girlband.*

Song: 'First of a New Genus'.

THE HYENAS.
I'm a lot for the world
Too much some say
But you've made me remember
Tomorrow's a new day
I won't shrink any more
Yeah I'll widen the door
For anyone who wants to come through

So I'll be the first of a new genus
A warrior of words
I'm heading back to the centre
Whoa whoaaa
Yeah I'm ready to change the world

And if it were easy
We'd be there already
Yeah if it were simple then
It wouldn't feel so deadly
But you're holding my hand
As I go take a chance
And I can feel your courage in my soullll

So I'll be the first of a new genus
A warrior of words
I'm heading back to the centre
Whoa whoaaa
Yeah I'm ready to change the world

MARY. London, 1787.

Chapter Ten: London, 1787

MARY *knocks on a door.* JOSEPH JOHNSON *answers.*

JOHNSON. Miss Wollstonecraft.

MARY. Mr Johnston.

JOHNSON. I was not expecting /

MARY. I'm ready for you to publish.

She thrusts her papers at him.

It's called *Thoughts on the Education of Daughters*. And it's the start of us changing the world.

I'm ready to change the world
Yeah I'm ready to change the world
Yeah I'm ready to change the world

Let's change the world, girls.

The clock ticks over, six days.

MARY *chucks* MARY S *a pen. Mic drop.*

ACT TWO

THE HYENAS *encircle* MARY, *impersonating the new men in her circle, while she sits and writes furiously.*

Underscore, 'We Are the Men'.

The MEN *introduce themselves as if they're reading out their Tinder bios. They are intellectual, flirty, buffoons.*

PAINE. Thomas Paine. American founding father, philosopher, revolutionary, with a dash of the debonair. Charmed.

GODWIN. William Godwin. Utilitarian, anarchist, anxious novelist. You're welcome.

FUSELI. Henry Fuseli. Swiss and sexxxy. Painter, posturer, practicer of depravity. I'm in your dreams, I'm in your *nightmares*. Call me.

He makes the phone gesture with his hands.

GENERIC MAN. Generic Man.

MARY *looks up from her writing only to give them one of her completed works.*

Song: *'We Are the Men'.*

MARY *thrusts out a finished manuscript.*

MARY. *Mary: A Fiction*

One of the chorus scoops it up.

MEN.
We are the Men
Most Important Men
Intellectual Men
Ahh and then there's Mary
Ahh and then there's Mary

MARY. *Original Stories From Real Life.*

Another manuscript.

MEN.
> She's writing like the devils on her back
> Writing like the bailiffs at her door
> Finally, a chance for some success
> Could be the key to somethin more
> All these famous minds are at her feet
> And everybody wants to know just how
> She's writing somethin no one ever speaks
> how / how / how?
>
> We are the Men
> Most Important Men
> Intellectual Men
> Ahh and then there's Mary
> Ahh and then there's Mary

MARY. *The Female Reader*

Another manuscript.

MEN.
> She sweats in ink and then she dreams on paper
> She never stops she knows she's gotta go
> She's on her own but really that's no bother
> No bother, no
> There's not a lot of time to make things good
> Not a lot of time for sisterhood
> She's doing somethin bigger than us all
> God forbid she makes a man feel small
>
> We are the Men
> Such Important Men
> Intellectual Men
> Oh and then there's Mary
> We are the Men
> Most Important Men
> Intellectual Men
> Ah and then there's Mary
> Ah and then there's Mary
> Ah and then there's Mary

EDMUND BURKE *steps forward – think Boris Johnson – brandishing a pamphlet.*

EDMUND BURKE. Edmund Burke. The OG Tory, writer of *Reflections on the Revolution in France* – spoiler – I'm not a fan. But I am a big success. And really who's going to challenge me?

MARY. Me!

She brandishes some writing of her own.

A Vindication of the Rights of Men. Vive la revolution! Take that Burke.

She bops him on his nose and horrified he scarpers. The chorus members start to carry her aloft. Chanting 'Mary, Mary, Mary, Mary.' She is triumphant.

The clock ticks over: five days.

They deposit her on the dinner table and take their places.

London, 1790.

Chapter Eleven: London, 1790

A dinner.

FUSELI. To the revolution – and its staunchest defender – Miss Wollstonecraft.

MARY. Well, I would never claim such a thing in the presence of Mr Paine /

FUSELI. Oh come now, Mary. You are the hero of the hour, don't shrink from it.

MARY. Don't tease, Fuseli.

FUSELI. I would never tease about you, Mary. I, at least, am forever in your orbit, whether the rest of the world follows or no.

For a second it seems as if he and MARY *are completely alone. She shakes it off but we can see he's got under her skin.*

JOHNSON. Have you read Mary's work, Thomas? It's been a huge success, knocked back Burke just when we needed it.

PAINE. Of course I've read it. It was an honour to do so, Miss Wollstonecraft.

MARY. I am the one that is honoured, Mr Paine.

FUSELI. Roscoe is commissioning a portrait you know. Mary immortalised. I suggested myself as the artist, but, there was some... reluctance.

MARY. My only *reluctance* was about your requests for how I should sit and in what attire.

JOHNSON. I imagine Mary is rather more attached to being fully clothed than your usual brand of model, Fuseli.

FUSELI. Regrettably so. Although I hope she is becoming more amenable to my view of the world. The aesthetic and sensual are not to be denied.

He caresses MARY. *We can see she is tempted. She almost leans in.*

JOHNSON. They are to be currently denied, or at least restrained. Or who knows where you would have us.

FUSELI. I do not find you that restrained, Johnson. At least not when we're alone.

His hands roam towards him. JOHNSON *shrugs him off.*

JOHNSON. We are not alone here.

FUSELI *winks at him.*

GODWIN. But when can we hear your response to Burke, Tom? We're all waiting. First is not necessarily best after all.

PAINE. It may take me a few months, I have not the lightning speed of Miss Wollstonecraft.

GODWIN. I think taking a little more care over its contents may be no bad thing.

MARY. I would very much like to hear where you hope the revolution will go? Will it follow America do you think? I hope it goes further.

PAINE. Oh? How?

MARY. Many ways. I really think women ought to have representatives.

PAINE. There is some sympathy without that position in America, although not widely voiced.

MARY. And you? What do you think, Mr Paine? Tell me honestly how can we be free citizens without having a direct share in the deliberations of government? It's indefensible, is it not?

PAINE. Mercy. Mercy please, Miss Wollstonecraft.

GODWIN. How can he tell you his thoughts? He can hardly squeeze a word in edgeways.

MARY. Excuse me?

GODWIN. You are not above thrusting yourself forward, Miss Wollstonecraft. I find it overbearing.

A pause.

MARY. *Overbearing.*

GODWIN. I didn't mean, I meant no offence.

MARY. I see.

She turns back.

Has it occurred to you, Mr Godwin, that the reason I appear '*overbearing*' is simply because you are used to members of my sex folding themselves into the background and deferring to male opinion? Because I am sure, I have spoken no more words than the rest tonight.

GODWIN. I am not objecting to your refusal to defer to male opinion, I am objecting to us not being able to hear that opinion, deference or not.

MARY. I am *sorry* you feel my voice is so loud to you. You're right of course, the world is sorely missing the *male* opinion.

JOHNSON. Now, Mary.

MARY. Do you frequently find your wife *overbearing*, Mr Godwin?

JOHNSON. Mary.

MARY. Men who argue passionately on the grounds of liberty and justice for all men often seem quite aghast at the suggestion that those who wash their socks and bear their children might also demand a look-in.

JOHNSON. Now come, Mary, a maid washes all our socks, yours too if I'm not mistaken, let's be fair.

GODWIN. I am not married. I find marriage to be a repulsive state.

MARY. As do I. Marriage is little better than slavery in my opinion.

GODWIN. Mine too.

MARY. Oh.

Their eyes hold for a second, they are surprised to agree.

FUSELI. Unity at last. Miss Wollstonecraft wants no man to tie her down, or tie her up, much to my disappointment. She is of the same mind as the pot beaters in Paris.

She turns from GODWIN.

MARY. As I would hope we all are, if we are defenders of freedom.

FUSELI. Such passion. And yet you would deny such fire from your own loins.

JOHNSON. Give the loins a rest, Fuseli.

GODWIN. It is logic and reason we must argue with, not passion surely. If we do not honour reason in all his might we are nowhere.

MARY. So reason is a man, is he?

GODWIN. It, well, I /

MARY. I think presuming logic and reason are male pursuits whilst looking at the world we live in, male-formed and much of it unjust, seems in itself quite illogical.

GODWIN. And you would argue a female one would be better?

MARY. I would argue a just world is an equal one. And that women cannot be judged by their output in this world, mistreated and subjugated as they are. Treat a human as little better than a beast and their intellect will become so.

FUSELI. I will happily treat you as a beast /

ALL. Shut up, Fuseli.

PAINE. It would seem the author of *The Rights of Man*, actually has quite a lot to say about *The Rights of Woman*.

MARY. Yes. Yes it would seem she does.

MARY gets up and leaves the table. It's time for the big one. She speaks to MARY S.

You know sometimes you don't even realise you're the only woman in the room until you look around for someone to catch your eyes and everyone is looking away.

MARY sits down to write. She goes to start but can't. Tries again, fails.

She summons her chorus of women: FANNY, ELIZA, EVERINA, MARY S.

How should I explain this to them? When they cannot understand. What it is to be born with a hand closed on your throat. When you cannot not even own your own heart unless it beats in another's fist. When you are taught to be nothing, ask for nothing, the degradation of it?

How can I make them see? Where should I start?

Song: 'Vindication of the Lives of Women'. MARY *speaks while* FANNY, ELIZA, EVERINA *and* MARY S *sing. Urging her to write for them.*

FANNY.
> They said I was delicate
> They'll remember me as weak

ELIZA.
> I follow etiquette

EVERINA.
> Nobody waits to hear me speak

FANNY.
> I travelled oceans to escape

ALL.
> My body is betrayed
>
> Vindication of the lives of women
> Yeah vindication of the things we've lost
> Of the things we could've been
> Of a race we'll never win
> Some things have their own specific cost

MARY has begun to write what they say, furiously.

MARY. I write anticipating every argument against me. I write as a duel to the death. Because, this, this is not just philosophy. This is not academic. This is life. This is our chance, slipping inky from my fingers and I must catch it. For all of us. I must.

ELIZA.
> You've got to tell everyone
> They have to know the things I've faced

EVERINA.
> The woman I could've been

ELIZA.
> We'll let the young be at the gates

FANNY.
> I travelled inside to escape

ALL.
> My body is betrayed

Vindication of the lives of women
Yeah vindication of the things we've lost
Of the things we could've been
Of a race we'll never win
Some things have their own specific cost

MARY *looks at* MARY S.

MARY. I write for you. In the future.

She looks at everyone.

I write for all of you. To excuse who we are. To make possible what you will become. To carve something better. Something bigger. Something.

And when will it change?
Really change / Really change
Vindication of the lives of women
Vindication of the lives of women
Vindication of the lives of women
Vindication of the lives of women

As the CHORUS *sings us out* MARY *holds up her manuscripts and speaks.*

MARY. I write because it is our chance. Our one and only chance. I write to breathe. To be seen. Known. Heard. Understood.

I write. I demand. I ask.

ALL.
Not for women to have power over men but over themselves.

She holds up the finished manuscript, nods at her chorus of women, and hands it to JOHNSON.

JOHNSON. Mary Wollstonecraft – *A Vindication of the Rights of Woman*. The publishers are waiting. This is big, Mary. This is really big. You're sure?

MARY. I have to be. For all of us.

Chapter Twelve

MARY *stands in the street. Holding her book. The* CHORUS *swirl around her.*

A STREET VENDOR *starts to chuck books about.*

STREET VENDOR. Roll up. Roll up. New stock. From the author of *Vindication of the Rights of Men*. It's a good one, lads. Yep Mary Wollstonecraft herself, getting your women out of the kitchen and into all sorts of trouble.

THE HYENAS *grab them. They begin to declaim as the critics.*

CRITICS. This is simply outrageous /

Preposterous.

Contagious.

Women asking for rights

What a horror

What a fright

Never heard something so ridiculous

Whoever wrote it must be monstrous

Better stamp on it – HARD.

Out of the throng three extra pompous CRITICS *step out. Think eyeglasses and canes. They pontificate.*

'Vindication of the Rights of Brutes', if women are to be equal why not brutes? Why not vegetables?

Perhaps the author would become more pleasing and infinitely happier if she should assume some of the feminine graces she despises.

She is one of a clan of desperate, wicked, and mischievously ingenious women, who are likely to bring ruin and shame upon all those who listen to them.

They start to circle MARY. *She bats them off.*

MARY. It's out there. It's out there in the world. That's what matters.

CRITICS. This is simply disgusting /

Revolting /

Maddening /

Women the equals of men /

And if we say it's true – What then?

Never heard something so frightening /

The author deserves a flogging /

Better stamp on her –

HARD

A hyena in petticoats.

Her best friends can never wish that her work should be remembered.

Horribly unfeminine. Deficient in method and arrangement.

MARY. Can you stop, stop please. Just for a second. I mean you've never met me. You've never even /

CRITICS. This is simply NOT THE WAY THINGS ARE DONE.

She's a joke

She a whore

She's an ugly little no one.

The voices begin to overlap and speed up until we can hardly tell who is speaking. She is crowded out. Hardly visible.

Sprawling, disorganised, uneven /

Hysterical, demanding, domineering /

Loud, absurd, ridiculous /

Bossy, hectoring, ugly /

Petty, self-important, demanding /

Dour, miserable, boring /

Aggressive. Emotional. Shrill.

Nasty.

A nasty woman.

Calm down, dear.

Watch your tone.

Stupid stupid woman

Lock. Her. Up.

Come on, boys

All together now

Better

Stamp

Stamp

Stamp

Stamp

On her

HARD.

MARY. PLEASE. STOP.

MARY runs from them. They laugh and then disperse. She lands at Fuseli's door.

She hesitates for a second. Looks at MARY S.

The great thing about being a woman is in your darkest hour you can always think of a man who can make you feel worse.

She knocks hard on the door. FUSELI *answers in a chic silk dressing gown, only just belted.*

FUSELI. Mary?

MARY. Can I come in?

FUSELI. What do you want?

MARY. I want. I. I don't know. I, I suddenly wanted to see you.

FUSELI. I thought you had made it clear you weren't interested. Have you changed your mind?

MARY. I wanted, I wanted someone to stand by me, now the rest of the world has changed course. And I thought you –

As he speaks he runs her hand down her body. Cups her chin. She almost folds into him.

The things they are saying about me. Have you heard? They think I'm a monster.

FUSELI You can be as monstrous as you like with me.

He tempts her. His hands probing.

MARY. You're married.

FUSELI. Yes.

MARY. But perhaps. We could be together. All of us.

FUSELI. Ménage à trois? Mary, you surprise me.

He goes to pull her close. She resists, breaking away.

MARY. Chastely. Chastely I mean. Perhaps we could live together. A meeting of minds.

FUSELI. Mary.

MARY. A partnership of souls only. If you truly value me, that is.

He is cold now.

FUSELI. And why would I care about your soul?

MARY. I… I thought –

FUSELI. I've made it clear what I want, Mary. If you can't give it to me I'm not interested.

MARY. Fuseli.

He shuts the door. MARY *quietly.*

Please.

I am. I am very lonely.

Forever in my orbit, I thought –

Please.

She sinks to the ground. Hugging her knees.

MARY S. Did that really happen? I always thought maybe he made it up. To make you seem desperate.

MARY. Funny what we think makes a woman look desperate. Is it shameful to admit I want to be loved? I want to be desired, and cherished? Yes. As well as be free. I do not want to be lonely forever. To feel that I am too much for the world, forever.

You see when I was writing I felt so sure of where I was going, and now I have nothing. I just feel empty.

JOHNSON *comes on carrying a suitcase.*

JOHNSON. He's never going to make you feel better, Mary.

MARY. I can't feel better anywhere. There is no place for me in this world.

JOHNSON. In France they are building a new world.

MARY. Yes. The revolution.

JOHNSON. How would you like to go and see?

MARY. France?

JOHNSON. Paris. You could report for the analytical review.

MARY. Go? To Paris? Be a part of the revolution?

JOHNSON. Yes.

MARY. Me? Yes! I mean yes I'll go. Of course I want to go.

JOHNSON. It will be dangerous, Mary.

MARY turns, picks up a suitcase.

Drums beat. 'La Marseillaise' plays.

KING LOUIS XVI walks forward, kneels.

MARY. Neck or nothing is the word.

MARY chops his head off. The clock ticks: four days.

Paris, 1792.

Chapter Thirteen: Paris, 1792

THÉROIGNE DE MÉRICOURT *bursts on the scene. A blood-red riding outfit and sabre at her side. Open jacket and breasts strapped. She takes two pistols from holsters, fires them into the air.*

THÉROIGNE DE MÉRICOURT. Time to get this party started, bitches.

Suddenly we are in a French salon. Famous female minds of the revolution are everywhere.

Party vibes. MARY *is swept up and thrown into the middle of it. Jostling, flashing lights, dancing, rebellion. We are drunk on freedom.*

HELEN. Mary.

MARY. Helen.

HELEN. Helen Williams, poet, correspondent, matchmaker.

She winks.

(*To* MARY.) We didn't know you were here already.

MARY. Yes, two weeks.

HELEN. How are you finding us?

MARY. It is very...

At this moment THÉROIGNE DE MÉRICOURT *gets out her sabre and spins on the dance floor. Shouting.*

THÉROIGNE DE MÉRICOURT. Les femmes devez prendre des armes!

MARY. French.

HELEN. That is because here we are ALIVE. You must meet everyone.

She swirls her round the dance floor, pointing out the different figures.

Théroigne de Méricourt, she is campaigning for mixed salons, and the right of women to take up arms as patriots.

THÉROIGNE DE MÉRICOURT. You would make a fine swordsman, strong shoulders.

HELEN. Olympe De Gouge, author herself.

OLYMPE DE GOUGE. Playwright, citizonne, woman.

HELEN. Madame Roland, our hostess. And networker extraordinaire.

MADAME ROLAND. Charmant.

THÉROIGNE DE MÉRICOURT *raises a jug of red wine above her head.*

THÉROIGNE DE MÉRICOURT. Freedom, liberté, égalitaté.

A cheer. She pours it down her face. They all drink a toast.

MARY. I have never felt myself to be too conventional before but here –

HELEN. Nonsense you'll fit right in.

She pours her a drink.

MARY. I don't normally / partake

HELEN. You're in Paris, Mary, loosen up. Speaking of which –

She makes a beckoning gesture with her finger.

I've got quite the gentleman here who can give you a taste of the sights.

MARY. Helen.

HELEN. No, honestly, he's been asking about you. He's American, I know, charming. He's an author too, nothing on you, but a passable novel, good views on women, he's here on business and he's utterly corset-looseningly gorgeous, which helps.

MARY. You haven't worn a corset in years.

HELEN. Exactly, darling. Have fun.

IMLAY *approaches and* HELEN WILLIAMS *disappears into the throng.*

Helen, that's not what I'm here for Hel /en

IMLAY. Quite an entrance, mademoiselle.

MARY. Well, I came to make a stir. Although I fear in this company I am easily outshone.

IMLAY. I must disagree I'm afraid.

MARY. No, you mistake me. That is a good thing. Never has it felt easier to be myself. It seems that here people will be expecting all that and more.

IMLAY. You far exceed what we were expecting, Miss Wollstonecraft.

MARY. I am sorry I didn't realise we had met?

IMLAY. Your friend Miss Williams told me we might have the pleasure of your company tonight. I have read *A Vindication* and was quite overwhelmed at the possibility of meeting its author.

MARY. She is playing cupid I see. Well, I am flattered. We have not been properly introduced so I am at a disadvantage in returning the compliment.

IMLAY. Imlay. Gilbert Imlay. Author, charmer, and, wait for it, male feminist. I know. I know. Thank me later.

MARY. Delighted to meet you, Mr Imlay.

IMLAY. The delight is all mine.

MARY. You flatter me.

IMLAY. Only as much as you deserve.

The chorus shout 'Vivre la République'.

Cheers and dancing.

Have you visited Paris before?

MARY. Never.

IMLAY. I was hoping you might do me the great honour of letting me show you the sights?

He holds out his arm. MARY *looks him up and down, he is very good looking.*

MARY. Well, I mean if you insist.

The song begins. IMLAY *sings to* MARY, *charming her.*

Song: 'Falling for You'.

IMLAY.
This city feels so exciting
Fresh and new
But there's nothing more inviting
Than the light I see in you

MARY. I do not require flattery, Mr Imlay.

IMLAY. No, but perhaps you might enjoy it?

IMLAY *winks at her.*

If you let me fall for you
If you let me fall for you
Out of everything we do
I promise it'll be worth it

They trip through Paris. He charms her. She decides whether to let herself believe.

MARY. I have come to work. To write.

IMLAY. You give so much to the world, Mary, your writing. But don't you also deserve something for yourself? Don't you also deserve love?

He takes her hand. She is flustered but tempted.

Things are really changing
And it's everything to me
But there's somethin in your eyes tonight
I've never seen

They run through the abandoned Versailles.

If you let me fall for you
If you let me fall for you
Out of everything we do
I promise it'll be worth it
I promise it'll be worth it

Pausing. Looking at the splendour. The song is nearly over, but vestiges of romance linger. The echo of a fairylight and piano.

MARY. I believe in God, Mr Imlay, in the commitments we must make to virtue. I would not like you to mistake me.

IMLAY. Of course. But perhaps together we could redefine what virtue looks like in our new world.

MARY. I am not interested in fleeting encounters.

IMLAY. Tell me what you need. I can be it. I can be yours, you just need to show me you want it.

Suddenly she kisses him. Long and slow. She is testing what it could be like.

The kiss develops. Hands start to wander. Particularly IMLAY's. His fingers start to work in a way that is surprising and exciting to MARY.

Perhaps the song returns as underscore, but this time a little more sensual and sexy.

MARY. To be loved

Fully

It's tempting

It's

She nearly comes but holds back. She stops him, really looks at him for a second.

BUT. This would mean changing what I believe in, changing who I am. You promise that you mean it? This isn't just flirtation? This is meaningful. Right? This is sanctified?

IMLAY *murmurs to her as he kisses and tempts her.*

IMLAY. I can be anything you want me to be.

She still hesitates. He stops, gestures to their surroundings.

Look around. Look where we are. The foundations of a world are changing. We can decide on who we are. We can decide on how to be together. A new set of laws. A new world order being born. It's up to you, Mary.

She decides. She's choosing him, fully. She grins, snogs him.

Maybe the song returns and they sing together for the first time.

If you let me fall for you
If you let me fall for you
Out of everything we do
I promise it'll be worth it
I promise it'll be worth it

They tumble into bed. Maybe we get a little sexy saxophone. Some fireworks.

The bed spins.

IMLAY *disappears and* MARY S *throws back the covers to reveal* MARY *flat out.*

MARY S. So?

MARY. What?

MARY S. Was it worth it?

MARY. What?

MARY S. Him. Choosing him.

MARY. For a bit.

MARY S. And then?

MARY. Then –

>MARY *gets out of bed and starts to strap on a bump.*
>
>Things get real.
>
>MARY *sits down to write with her pregnant belly.*
>
>*The clock ticks: three days.*
>
>France. 1793.

Chapter Fourteen: Paris, 1793

IMLAY *is arguing with* MARY, *she tries to ignore him.*

IMLAY. I have asked you not to.

MARY. I know.

IMLAY. And yet you continue. You insist.

MARY. My work is the most important thing. You seemed to understand that when we met.

IMLAY. Things have changed.

MARY. The importance of this moment has not changed.

IMLAY. Of course it has! Of course it has, Mary. People are being dragged from their homes, our friends are imprisoned. The times have turned.

MARY. I must record what is happening.

IMLAY. You'll meet the guillotine if they find one hint of those papers.

MARY. I am prepared.

IMLAY. And what of your 'small creature'? Are you prepared for their sake too?

MARY *touches her stomach*.

MARY. That is not fair.

IMLAY. Isn't it?

MARY. You are just worried I will bring attention to your smuggling.

IMLAY. I would prefer it if you didn't draw quite so much attention yes. For both our sakes.

MARY. When we first met you led me to believe you liked the way I could draw attention.

IMLAY. The situation is different now, women with loud mouths are not so appreciated.

MARY. So that is how you see me, and my work? A woman with too loud a mouth.

IMLAY. Mary.

MARY. Women started this revolution. Women with loud mouths.

IMLAY. Yes and now their heads are being parted from their bodies for much less. I am just trying to protect you, Mary.

She really looks at him, tries to believe it.

MARY. If that is truly it, then… There is talk of a new decree. Now England has declared war. All English citizens in Paris must register.

IMLAY. I know.

MARY. I thought, I thought perhaps, if we were to register me as your wife I could go by Mrs Imlay. Then I would be American and we, me and the baby, we would be in no danger.

IMLAY. You want to be married? I thought you were always opposed.

MARY. No. I am. I am just saying if we were to register, to pretend /

IMLAY. I see.

MARY. But, only if. I am determined two people should only be together if they choose. To be bound spiritually, as we are, means more than any paper. But it would be a way for both of us to stay here and be safe.

IMLAY. It makes sense.

MARY. And you do choose us, Gilbert? It is what you want?

IMLAY. Why would you ask me that?

MARY. I, I just want to be sure. I am risking a lot for you. And it feels worth it because I can feel our future so clearly. But lately you, I worry that you do not feel the same.

IMLAY. I do. I have told you so many times that I do.

MARY. It could feel exciting. The best of both worlds. A way to be together without any of the yoke of tradition. Gilbert? At least I hope you do not see us as a yoke.

IMLAY. We'll register you tomorrow.

MARY. Right.

IMLAY. And then, I have to be away for business for a while.

He goes to leave.

MARY. Gilbert?

IMLAY. Do not fuss, Mary. This is what I mean. I will not be gone long.

He leaves. MARY *turns to* MARY *S.*

MARY. I think he meant it. When he said it. I don't think he knew /

MARY S. Don't you?

MARY. France. 1793. The Terror.

Chapter Fifteen: France, 1793. The Terror

THE HYENAS *dance. All the* WOMEN *we met earlier at the Salon are there dressed as if attending one of the famous 'bals des victimes', red lines across their necks, chains on their hands.*

They dance to 'La Guillotine Permanente'. The guillotine rises through the stage.

One of THE HYENAS *stands before it trembling with their red neck.*

We can't tell if this is pageantry or for real.

MARY *stares at it. She is really pregnant now. Ready to burst.*

The CHORUS *crowd her, singing.*

The FIGURE *kneels.* MARY *turns and tries to push her way back out of the crowd.*

MARY. Excuse me please. Execusez moi. Out of my way.

I feel a little faint please, could you.

The sound of the singing swells and grows. She becomes more desperate.

Please. Excusez moi. Air, I just need a little.

The PRISONER *begins to pray.*

Please. Excusez moi. Excusez moi.

Crowd crescendo. A cheer. A thud. For a second, silence, it has happened. MARY *faces away catching her breath.*

A head rolls down the stage. The CHORUS *pick it up and stick it on their poles. Laughing and cheering.*

MARY *clutches her stomach and leans down. She is sickened and in pain.*

MARGUERITE *comes up behind her.*

MARGUERITE. Marguerite Fournee, nurse, maid, citozene, hero. About to save the day. Excusez moi – (*She gestures to one of* THE HYENAS.) Hold my beret.

She marches up to MARY W.

Non non, vous devez faire semblant que vous aimez ca.

MARY. Pardonne?

MARGUERITE. English?

MARY. Yes. No! No sorry I mean American.

MARGUERITE. It is not safe for you to be here. They are killing English.

MARY. American.

MARGUERITE. Yes but –

MARY. Yes.

MARY *clutches her stomach in pain.*

One of the CHORUS *announces: 'The traitor Olympe de Gouges'. As* OLYMPE *mounts the platform in front of the guillotine. They cheer again, baying for blood.*

No.

MARGUERITE. They will be doing it for hours now, twenty-one they did yesterday.

MARY. I know her.

MARGUERITE. They say she is a monster who has forgot her natural place.

MARY. I've been to her salon.

MARGUERITE. Don't say that where they can hear you. Anyone on that side of the revolution is a traitor now. You are Jacobin or dead.

OLYMPE *begins to speak. It rings out.*

OLYMPE. La Femme naît libre et demeure égale à l'homme en droits. La femme a le droit de monter sur l'échafaud; elle doit avoir également celui de monter à la tribune.

[*Woman is born free and remains the equal of man in rights. If woman is entitled to mount the scaffold; she must be equally entitled to mount the rostrum.*]

Maybe MARGUERITE *translates some of this to us as she speaks. Maybe not.*

MARY. She is brave.

MARGUERITE. Easy to be brave when you have no chance of living. Up until then better to be smart, come on.

MARY *clutches her stomach and cries a little again.* OLYMPE *kneels.*

Why are you here?

MARY. I have run out of firewood, and bread. My husband, he has, he is gone, he has not sent money for a while.

MARGUERITE. Yes, well, I find when husbands are gone they are gone for good.

MARY. No. He will come back. Business. He will come back, before the baby is born.

MARY *gasps again and bends double.*

MARGUERITE. I do not think so. Unless he comes right now.

MARY. What?

MARGUERITE. That baby is coming. We need to get you somewhere safe. Your name?

MARY. Sorry?

MARGUERITE. Your name? What is your name?

MARY. Oh, Mary. Mary Woll– Imlay. Mary Imlay.

MARGUERITE. Marguerite. I'm a maid – well, not at the minute, at the minute short of employments – but in normal times.

MARY. Ah hu ahahahahahaha.

MARGUERITE. Ok. Ok breathe.

MARY. Ahhhhhh. Gilbert.

MARGUERITE. Mary this baby is coming. We are doing this now.

MARY. He will come. I know he will come.

MARGUERITE. Breathe. I need you to breathe for me.

MARY. Ahhhhhhhhhhhhhhhhahhahaah. He will come.

MARGUERITE. If you say so.

MARY. Ahhhhhh.

MARGUERITE. Push.

MARY. Ahhhhhhhhhhhhhhhhhhhhhhh. Gilbert. Where. Are. You??

OLYMPE *says her last words.*

OLYMPE. Enfants de la Patrie, vous vengerez ma mort!

The axe falls and OLYMPE*'s head rolls.*

The stage runs with blood.

Marguerite delivers Fanny.

For a second everything stops. Mary holds her.

MARGUERITE. A little girl.

MARY. My. My little girl.

MARGUERITE. Her name?

MARY. Fanny. Fanny Imlay.

MARGUERITE. Really? For her father?

MARY. For my friend. The bravest woman I have ever known.

Maybe we hear a little tinkle of 'Find Your Tribe Here'. After a second MARGUERITE *gently tries to probe.*

MARGUERITE. He's not coming back, is he, Mary? Even for her.

MARY *shakes her head, won't listen, gets up with baby Fanny and starts to pack.*

MARY. He's written. He wants to come.

MARGUERITE. Oh he's written.

MARY. He says he's lost the money. Everything he had saved. It's sailed off on a ship to Sweden and if I can just find it /

MARGUERITE. Mary. You can't be serious?

MARY *picks up her suitcase and the baby.*

MARY. I'm going. If I can just find it, he says we can be together. A family.

MARGUERITE. This is mad. They say the French are mad, but this /

MARY. It's an adventure.

MARGUERITE. I have lived through a revolution I don't need more adventure.

MARY. He needs the money. We need the money, if we're going to have a life together.

MARGUERITE. If he cared, Mary. Truly. He would go himself. He would have been here months ago. If he was any sort of man at all.

MARY. I chose him, Marguerite. I choose him still. I've staked everything on this, my integrity, morality, my heart. I have to make this work.

MARY *steps onto the ship with* MARGUERITE *and little Fanny. Standing at its prow.*

We hear a few chords of the song.

HYENA. We call this one: 'Sometimes Even Feminism Isn't Enough to Keep You from a Fuckboy'.

Song: 'Sometimes Even Feminism Isn't Enough to Keep You from a Fuckboy'.

The song begins for real.

Sometimes
Feminism just isn't enough
To keep a girl from wanting love
You know he's a dickhead
You know he's a liar
But sometimes a love can just set you on fire

The sounds of the sea and the ship start to mix with the song. It's pretty wild, a storm gathering.

Just say you love me
I won't give up for nothin'
I've given you everythin'
Don't start running

MARY *stands holding baby Fanny, on the prow of a ship. Windswept. It lurches and blows but she is firm. Maybe a rumble of thunder.*

You can really argue and you can shout
You can try and reason beyond doubt
You know he's not clever
You know he's not wise
But it's a little too painful to watch a love that dies

Just say you love me
I won't give up for nothin'
I've given you everything
Don't start running

The storm gets worse. They cling on to the railings. The singing fighting to be heard above the noise, but it is starting to disintegrate.

You get to thinkin' this time, well maybe
Then it's you left holding the baby

And if you cling on too hard
And if you demand
You know you just wanted him to hold your hand

In the distance from somewhere very far away IMLAY *looks at her.* MARY *looks at him. Desperate.*

Just say you love me
I won't give up for nothin'
I've given you everything
Don't start running
Just say you love me
I won't give up for nothin'
I've given you everything
Don't starrrrrttttt, running.

The storm becomes too much, interrupting the song. IMLAY *turns and starts to walk away.*

MARY. No. No, don't go, don't.

She tries to keep the song going over the raging storm.

Just say you love me
I won't give up for nothin
I've given you everything
Don't start running

He is gone. She shouts after him.

I won't give up! Do you hear me? I won't.

Just say you love me
I won't give up for nothin
I've given you everything
Don't start running
Don't start –

And in years to come people will belittle me.
Call me clingy or needy.
For demanding you show up. Keep your promises.
For demanding you remember, love.
Remember us.
But I won't be judged.

A flash of lightning, climax of the storm. The ship lurches. Finally, she falls.

MARGUERITE. Mary.

MARGUERITE *makes her way up the ship. Holds onto her.*

MARY. The money is gone. I can't find it. And he. He. He's not coming.

MARGUERITE. You've hurt your head.

MARY. I so wanted to do it. I so wanted to prove I was worth it.

MARGUERITE. You are. You are. You hear me? He is not worth you. You can't make people be better than they are. This is one thing even Mary Wollstonecraft cannot do.

MARY. What do we do now?

MARGUERITE. We go home. We go to dry fucking land and forget him. You see.

Time ticks over: two days.

MARY. London, 1795.

Chapter Sixteen: London, 1795

IMLAY*'s house in London.*

IMLAY. I wasn't expecting you to come here.

MARY. Who is she?

IMLAY. I will pay, for lodgings, for Fanny. I will pay for you to be kept decently, I won't see you destitute.

—

I didn't expect you to come here, Mary. You can't be here.

MARY. Who is she, Gilbert?

IMLAY. I made it clear that my feelings had changed. I made it clear before I left France even.

MARY. *'Business alone has kept me from you. Come to any port and I will fly down to my two girls with a heart all their own.'*

IMLAY. You harassed me, Mary. I didn't know how to calm you, but the truth is you have driven me away. With your demands, and your moods. The truth is my feelings have been changed for a long time. I think you have known that.

MARY. Who is she?

IMLAY. I will not be made to feel guilty. I am a free man. You were always clear on that. Not to be tied down. Keep our freedoms. You were always clear.

MARY. Not to chain each other, oppress each other, yes. But I consider myself bound to you, you know that. You knew that I was facing judgement about our choices, about our –

You knew it was different for me.

IMLAY. I will not be made to feel guilty.

MARY. I have a right to know who she is. I have a right to know who has destroyed all my hopes. Who? I have a right, Gilbert. Please.

IMLAY. She is an actress.

MARY. I see.

IMLAY. She is much admired in town. Everyone is talking of her latest performance.

MARY. Is everyone welcoming her into their bedroom as well or is that just you?

IMLAY. I won't have her disrespected, Mary.

MARY. You dare to talk to me of disrespect. You dare.

IMLAY. It is over between us. How can I make you understand that?

MARY. I have trekked halfway across the world for you. I have borne ships, and storms, and days, days where I did not know what I would do with Fanny. Where she cried on the road and I longed to scream. And days where I was away from her. Where I left her with Marguerite and tore out my own heart to go without her. I missed things. Her smiles and her words and her steps. For you. So you would love me.

IMLAY. And yet you have returned with nothing.

MARY. I have weaned Fanny. Taken her mouth from my breast. Because I thought you might, so I would be ready for you if you wanted –

IMLAY. What happened to you, Mary? I thought I fell in love with a woman of fire? Of independence and sparkle and wit. And you became nothing more than a nag. You clung to me so hard it made me sick.

MARY. You! You happened. You take my fire and then scorn me that it is gone? Oh what a man. What a big big man you are.

IMLAY. I need you to leave.

MARY. I have nowhere to go.

IMLAY. I will honour my commitments to my child but you must go.

MARY. She is my child. MINE. My little girl, that I have loved and grown and cherished and fed and held and bathed and fought for. She is mine. I want her to know nothing of you. Nothing. Do you hear me?

IMLAY. Goodbye, Mary.

MARY *starts to walk through London in the rain.*

MARY S *follows her. She calls out, but she can't reach her.*

MARY S. Mary. Mary, where are you going?

MARY *murmurs to herself, perhaps we hear an echo of the song.*

MARY.
> **So just say you love me**
> **I'm ready to be nothing**
> **I've given you everything**
> **Can't keep running.**

MARY stands on top of Putney Bridge. She walks up and down, up and down, again and again. Making her dress wet and heavy.

THE HYENAS' impersonation of her critics returns. Ringing loud in her ears.

'Desperate. Wicked. Ruin. Shame.' (Repeated.)

We begin to hear 'A Little Patience'.

She climbs the railings. She looks out at the world.

She pauses.

MARY. There is no new world, is there? Only the old one again and again and again.

MARY S calls to her desperately.

MARY S. That's not true. That's not true there is. You're helping to make it. Remember? You're helping to make it for me.

MARY. A fire burning in the pit of my stomach. It says this is wrong. They are wrong. But what if I am wrong? Made wrong? Just as everyone seems to think.

MARY S. You're not wrong, Mary? Mum? You're not wrong. Please. Please hang on for me.

MARY S starts to run, trying desperately to reach her.

You can't go yet. You can't go yet, can you. It's not time yet. We've still got days. It's not the right time.

Another echo of the song.

> **Another life wasted another hope lost**
> **I open my eyes and we're back to the start**
> **A woman betrayed by the beat of her heart**

A moment of calm. MARY *thinks.*

MARY. A little patience and all will be over.

She jumps.

The world turns. Revolves. For a second she is suspended.

She lands in the water.

One long cry that combines with the FUCCCKKKKKKKK of the song.

MARY S. No!

Stop. Darkness.

MARY S *walks to the water. Slowly she pulls her out, cradles her and begins to sing.*

Song: 'You Can't Always Be the Strong Woman'.

Ever find yourself wondering
Every road that you're going
Can you be the strong woman?
Yeah we need a strong woman
But the weight of that sayin'
Yeah we're always downplayin'
Just to feel the earth turnin'
When the fire ain't burnin'

And every hand is on your chest
Every day another test

Sometimes – just sometimes
You can't always be the strong woman
Sometimes – just sometimes
It's ok just to be a woman
Fully flawed fucked up woman
And when I'm unsure of this road I'm goin
Catch me when I fall

When they tell me I'm fearless
Yeh I know they can't hear us
Cos everything's crushing

It makes me feel nothing
Cos I'm soft and I'm gentle
Let me be sentimental
Doesn't mean I'm not fire
To be burnt by desire

And everyone will say the same
Yeah it's her that we blame

Sometimes – just sometimes
You can't always be the strong woman
Sometimes – just sometimes
It's okay just to be a woman
Fully flawed fucked-up woman
And when I'm unsure of this road I'm goin'
Catch me when I fall

Instrumental.

Catch me when I fall... (*Fade.*)

As MARY S *sings* MARY *is lovingly carried to Johnson's house.*

They put her back into bed in a way which mirrors the fever scene from the beginning. MARY S *carefully tucks her in.*

Chapter Seventeen

MARGUERITE, JOHNSON *and baby Fanny come in, gather around* MARY *in a makeshift bed.*

JOHNSON. Mary? Mary, are you awake?

Startled MARY *looks around.*

You're safe. You're safe here.

MARY. Fanny? Fanny?

JOHNSON. She's here. Marguerite's got her, she's here.

MARGUERITE. You fool. You stupid fool.

MARGUERITE *places Fanny in* MARY*'s arms.*

MARY. I'm sorry. I'm so so sorry. Oh God I'm sorry.

JOHNSON. It's okay. It's okay. We've got you. We've got you.

MARY. I just felt, I just suddenly felt –

JOHNSON. Yes.

MARY. I wasn't sure I could do it any more. I couldn't, I, I wasn't, and I thought Fanny would be better without me. I thought maybe everything would just be better without me.

MARGUERITE. Nothing would be better without you.

JOHNSON. You're safe. Two men saw you jump. They pulled you out the water.

MARGUERITE. We've been waiting for you to wake up so we could kill you again.

JOHNSON. Marguerite.

MARY. Imlay?

JOHNSON. We haven't heard anything, Mary.

MARY. Does he know?

MARGUERITE. Yes. But he hasn't come. I'm sorry.

—

JOHNSON. Are you, how do you feel?

MARY. Please do not write to my sisters about this. Please don't tell anyone.

JOHNSON. No.

MARY. I wouldn't want Fanny to think, I wanted to stay, I wanted to stay for her. I just thought, I don't know. I just wasn't sure I could keep doing it.

MARGUERITE. He is bastard.

JOHNSON. You will get over this, Mary. You will get over him. It is a great disappointment, one you do not deserve, but you will get through it.

MARGUERITE. Yes. We will make sure.

JOHNSON. All of us. You must stay here until you are well. Mary? You will be well again.

—

MARY. I know it. I think I just need a little time. Thank you. Thank you for holding on to me.

They leave. MARY *looks over to* MARY S.

How long left?

The clock ticks over: one day. They both look at it.

MARY S. Not long. Can you do this next bit?

MARY. I'd better, hadn't I? After all it's the bit that gets me you.

MARY S *helps her out of bed. Sits at her desk, gives her a pen. She looks at her hard.*

MARY S. How do you do it?

MARY. What?

MARY S. Be well again.

MARY. I write.

She starts to scribble.

Letters Written During a Short Residence in Sweden, Norway, and Denmark.

She pauses writing and looks up.

London, 1796.

Chapter Eighteen: London, 1796

JOHNSON *ushers* GODWIN *into the room.*

JOHNSON. Mary? I did say that you were not as yet accepting visitors. But Mr Godwin insisted.

GODWIN. I hope you do not mind the intrusion, Miss Wollstonecraft.

MARY. Mrs Imlay.

GODWIN. Imlay? Still?

MARY. Still. Otherwise my child is a bastard, Mr Godwin, and I would not condemn her.

GODWIN. Yes. Quite, I didn't mean /

MARY. I am working.

GODWIN. Yes, I can see that. I will not take up much of your time.

MARY *thinks about it. She isn't excited but she acquiesces.*

MARY. Of course.

JOHNSON. I will leave you both to it.

He leaves.

Pause. GODWIN *is awkward.*

MARY. I am sorry not to be more welcoming. My writing time is precious now, with little Fanny I have to guard what moments I can snatch.

GODWIN. I can imagine.

Pause. GODWIN *is working up to something.*

I wanted to say, I am not always the best expressing my thoughts in conversation, but I really wanted to make clear how much I enjoyed *Letters from Sweden and Norway*.

MARY. Thank you.

GODWIN. I honestly felt, I don't know reading it. It is a work of such delicate sensibility and vision. I felt you had provided us with a window to your soul, and that was, to make such a piece of art out of such heartbreak. It was very brave. To be such a person who could write something so... it was almost enough to make you fall in love as you read it.

—

MARY. I did not think you were a great fan of my work, Mr Godwin.

GODWIN. No. No I imagine you did not.

MARY. I am familiar with yours of course, *Political Justice* I read with interest.

GODWIN. Thank you.

MARY. I seem to remember you were less enamoured with my *Vindications*.

GODWIN. It is true that I, honestly in parts I found them confronting and the style I felt perhaps was, less to my taste. But, I think I was hasty perhaps in my opinions. I, I suspect both of us may have been mellowed by experience in the years since.

MARY. It is true that certain, experiences, in the years since have changed me. As any great emotional turbulence will do.

GODWIN. I can sympathise.

MARY. But I do not feel this has made me any less steadfast in my convictions.

GODWIN. Of course. So I would hope. And I would hope that you might accept an offer of support from a matured and improved old friend.

Pause. She thinks. She is not going to jump this time.

MARY. Perhaps.

GODWIN. And perhaps, one day, you might consider the possibility of an old friend becoming something more?

MARY. I have fought hard to carve out my space in this world. I will not let someone shrink it again. For my sake. Or for Fanny's.

GODWIN. What if there were to be someone who might help you with the carving?

MARY. Does such a man exist?

GODWIN. When we spoke about marriage, all those years ago, I have always remembered it.

MARY. Yes.

GODWIN. As the years have gone on I have recognised that to have a companion who can match you in values, who strives to live to their own standards, that is something exceptional.

MARY. Is it perhaps easier to contemplate my values now I am a little broken Mr Godwin? I take up less space. But I want someone who, would love me for my stridency not only my soft edges. I have made that mistake before.

Silence. Then very quietly GODWIN *says –*

GODWIN. I think I would love you for your courage.

MARY *looks at him. Moved.*

MARY S. What are you thinking?

MARY. I'm thinking do I dare. One last experiment. Maybe?

Reprise, 'Utopian Dreams'. Softly it grows underneath the action.

FANNY *tumbles in.* MARY *watches* GODWIN *try to entertain her. She trips him up. Dresses him up. Plays hide and seek.*

Fondness is a poor substitute for friendship. Possession is a poor mate for life.

A marriage of equals is all that I ask, I won't mute myself to be a wife.

GODWIN. Of course. I, I wouldn't expect you to.

MARY *rips through the house. Throwing things out of her way.* GODWIN *scurries behind. Trying to catch them.*

MARY. I won't be left to clean your mess.
 I won't be abandoned with domestic tasks.
 I won't be reduced to another's drudge.
 I won't be shrugged off, belittled, or ignored.

GODWIN tries to keep up with the tasks she sets him. These can be modern. Hoovering. Washing up. Cooking. He is not very good but he is giving it a go. Rubber gloves and all.

GODWIN. Mary / I

MARY. If it's our house
 It's ours
 But my time
 Is not yours.
 Not this time.
 Not this time.

GODWIN. Okay.

MARY. Okay?

GODWIN. Okay. A marriage of equals. We don't know if it's even possible. A partnership. But I'll get better at it. I'm willing to try. Honestly.

Pause, she looks at him, rubber-gloved hand outstretched.

Mary?

MARY. Alright. Let's give it a try.

She lets him sweep her off her feet.

London, 1797.

They end up...

Chapter Nineteen: London, 1797

MARY *and* GODWIN *sit at their writing desks side by side working.*

MARY *heavily pregnant again.*

GODWIN. Do you plan to dine with us tonight, Mary?

MARY. Perhaps.

GODWIN. Keeping me on my toes.

MARY. I am desperate to finish this chapter.

GODWIN. I see.

MARY. Time seems ever shorter now I know I am to be incapacitated so soon and I have so much still to say, so much still to do.

GODWIN. Little Fanny would give you even less time, she wants the baby here already. She is most excited for a little brother or sister.

MARY. I know. I know.

GODWIN. It is going well? You have been very quiet on its subject.

MARY. I hope so. It is knotty, but, I thought of a title today. *Maria: or, the Wrongs of Woman.*

GODWIN. That is a subject you know more than a little about.

MARY. Yes. Yes I thought that too.

GODWIN *kisses her head and leaves.*

MARY *returns to her scribbling.*

We watch her for a while.

MARY *gets up and her and* MARY S *start to circle each other again.*

MARY S. You never get chance to end it, *The Wrongs of Woman*.

MARY. No. But maybe one of you will.

The clock ticks over, finally zero.

We are transformed, back to the start.

Epilogue

MARY S. The day my mother died a comet shot across the sky.

HYENA. Nothing like that had been seen in a lifetime. It was like the future. The future was blazing in front of us.

HYENA. London's clouds turned blood red /

MARY S. The world held its breath and /

MARY. You. Mary Wollstonecraft Shelley was born.

Finally they reach out. Hands holding. Whirling each other around. The chorus start to creep onstage and surround them.

MARY. I still had so much to do. So much to change.

MARY S. I'm sorry.

MARY. Know that I love you. Won't you? I love you and your sister. I love you so so much.

MARY S. We know.

MARY. Live a full life. Don't ever let them tell you you can't. Live it all. Love. Sex. Politics. Ideals. Have ideals. Have morals. Think for yourself. Never be afraid of being too much. Feel wildly. Deeply. Richly. Think. Big thoughts. Huge. The world needs them.

MARY S. I'll try.

They hold each other.

MARY. What happens?

MARY S. What?

MARY. After. To you. To all of you? Was it worth it? Do we change anything? Anything at all? Tell me. Tell me please.

MARY S. So much. So so much.

> MARY *steps out onto a plinth. It begins to rise again. Through the ages. Pushing her forward. To now. To today.*

> *The clock starts to spin forwards, dates again now: 1797, 1818, 1882, 1918, 1928, 1975, 1991, 2010, faster and faster, until it eventually lands on today.*

We read everything you left behind. We trace its echoes through the ages. We dissent. We rebel. We hear your voice.

> *From her plinth* MARY *chucks down her a pen. She holds it aloft.*

In me. Mary Shelley. Author. Writer. Mother. Visionary. Inventor of science fiction. Who lives her own extraordinary life, battling misogyny and society and men who just should have known fucking better.

MARGARET. In me. Margaret Kingsborough. Who escapes her marriage and absconds to Germany to train as a doctor disguised as a man. And who, years later, will catch your daughter at her lowest ebb in Italy and give her back to herself. Just like she did as a little girl for you all those years ago.

> *They pass the pen between them as each move forward. Moving us through time. To now.*

ELIZA/EVERINA. In us.

ELIZA. Eliza /

EVERINA. And Everina.

ELIZA. Who start another school in Ireland.

EVERINA. And who will never admit their pride, but who often tell people who their sister was.

ELIZA. What she achieved. What she stood for.

MARGUERITE. In me, Marguerite. Who looks after your girls for years. Who protects them as fiercely as she can from a world that tries to steal their power.

FANNY. And in me, Fanny. Who tries so hard to be happy. Who tries so hard, but ultimately cannot. Who takes a laudanum overdose, and is found alone, dead, in underwear marked 'MW', as a reminder of what we are fighting to prevent and how far we still have to go.

HYENAS. And in more, so many more /

In Sojourner Truth, who escapes slavery and dares to stand up and ask 'Ain't I a Woman'?

And who might have taught even you a thing or two about oppression and the breadth of womanhood.

And Millicent Fawcett, marching with the suffragettes and citing you as their foremother /

And Virginia Woolf tracing your influence in that room of her own /

And bell hooks carving her own revolutionary path /

And George Eliot defending your name /

And Audre Lorde /

And Toni Morrison /

And us.

In all of us. Who hear your voice, who stand up for our rights. Who continue the struggle. Here today.

Once you wrote:

MARY. 'I cannot bear to think of being no more – it appears to me impossible that I should cease to exist.'

HYENAS. Well, know this. It was impossible. Because here you are now. Now still.

Because your story is a story for all women who blaze before their time.

Because you begin a revolution that is still ongoing.

MARY. *A Vindication for the Rights of Women.*

ALL. A vindication for us all!

MARY stands tall on her plinth. Suddenly she is bathed in a silvery light.

She begins to sing. To summon her army. We all hear her call and join in. Moving, speaking, calling together.

Song: Reprisal 'How Do You Grow A Girl'/'Vindication of the Lives of Women'.

Ohhhhhh
How do you grow a girl?
How do you raise them?
Protect them
Save them
How do you make it fair?
In an unfair world
In an unfair world

But, they can change the world
Tell them
They can change the world
Teach them
They can change the world
Teach them
They can change the world
It's time
We changed the world
It's time

Vindication of the lives of women
Vindication of the path we tread
The example of all of us
Blazes in front of us
Remember us when we're dead

MARY. I do not ask for women to have power over men, but over themselves. KEEP ASKING.

Fists punch the air.

The End.

Acknowledgements

It's a bit cliché to say that it takes a village to make a play, but it really does and, truly, there are so many people who helped make this script what it is. Thank you so much every single one of you, for all you have given me and Mary.

Some specific thanks:

To Mark and Tom at Hull Truck Theatre, who believed in this idea right from the off and helped nurture it to its first beginnings. To Esther, who cut to its heart immediately, and carried it with such care and boldness and bravery. To Laura, who lived and breathed Mary's voice and helped us keep that close. To all the original cast who gave something of themselves with such generosity. To the creative team and staff teams at Hull Truck and Pilot, you are all wonders. To my brilliant agent Giles, who fought my fights when I needed them and made it all possible. To my mum, who first introduced me to Mary and showed me what it looked like to carve your own extraordinary path. To my partner, Dec, who holds my hand when it all gets too much. To anyone I've cried on, argued with, or monologued at about the show. And lastly to Mary – what a woman. Thank you.

M.L.

Learning Resources and Activities

Written by Carolyn Bradley
Edited by Oliver O'Shea

These resources may be of particular interest to those teaching: Drama and Theatre Studies (KS3-KS5); English (KS3-KS5); the French Revolution for A level History (KS5); and liberalism for A level Politics (KS5).

The resources explore the life and historical context of Mary Wollstonecraft, and can be used to help students understand the story and themes of the play.

> We have included prompt questions to help students engage with the play; these appear in shaded panels, like this one.

We would suggest that you consider whether any of the subjects explored in the play and resources may be triggering for some of your students, and we advise that the resources contain plot spoilers.

Originally developed with the support of Arts Council England and the Keith Howard Foundation.

Who was Mary Wollstonecraft?

Mary Wollstonecraft was a radical writer and philosopher, known for her early feminist views and advocacy for equality between men and women. In eighteenth-century Europe, she challenged convention by campaigning for the education of girls so that they could contribute more fully to society, arguing that women were not inferior to men but that they were limited by their lack of education and opportunities.

In early adulthood, she took on traditional feminine roles as a lady's companion, governess and teacher, before establishing herself as a writer. She worked as a writer, reviewer and translator for the radical publisher Joseph Johnson in London, further challenging convention by being financially self-sufficient with a career. She believed in the philosophy of classical liberalism and supported the French Revolution, travelling to France during this time and writing about it. She wrote fiction, conduct guides, political pieces and children's stories, but is most known today for her work *A Vindication of the Rights of Woman* published in 1792.

In the final year of her life, she married fellow radical and early anarchist William Godwin and was the mother of Mary Shelley, who became the author of *Frankenstein*.

Mary Wollstonecraft and Feminism

What is Feminism?

Feminism is the belief in true social, political and financial equality between the sexes, advocating for women to receive the same opportunities and rewards as men. Feminism is a worldwide response to the gender-based oppression of women throughout history. Historically, women have not had the right to vote, to own property, to attend university, study medicine, to receive birth control, or even to receive a basic education.

Mary's Feminist Beliefs

From an early age, Mary believed in equal rights for the sexes and individualism, and as a child was frustrated at her lack of status and opportunities, compared to her brother Ned. For example, Ned went to a boys' grammar school with access to a library and wide range of subjects and activities, whereas Mary went to a small village school and would have studied little more than reading and writing. Ned was entitled to inherit from his grandfather, and Mary was not. Ned was able to graduate into a career as a lawyer, Mary was not entitled to any such path.

She witnessed her mother's abuse at the hands of her alcoholic father and nursed her mother before her death in her early fifties. Much about her mother's life would have fuelled Mary's determination not to experience a similar fate.

In her letters and stories, Mary was critical of the need for women to dress attractively for men, to do their hair and wear make-up, or to wear corsets and petticoats. When working as a companion in Bath, she wrote critically about the girls who were obsessed with fashion; as a governess for the Kingsboroughs, she was critical of Caroline, Lady Kingsborough, for wearing too much rouge, bathing in milk and caring more about her pet dogs than educating her children.

In one letter to Jane Arden, she wrote: 'It is a happy thing to be a mere blank, and to be able to pursue one's own whims, where they lead, without having a husband and half a hundred children at hand to tease and control a poor woman who wishes to be free.'

Mary wanted to be financially independent, not have to find a husband for security and had no interest in the 'traditional' feminine pursuits of needlecraft, music and sewing. However, although she shunned marriage until later in life, she still found herself in the traditional feminine roles of lady's companion, governess and teacher, as no other options were available to her. In her writing, she criticised the lack of independence women had in society. This all changed when she met the publisher

Joseph Johnson, a like-minded radical, who employed her as a writer and allowed her to live alone and work, breaking the mould for eighteenth-century women.

Mary had unconventional views towards sex, marriage and children which were not widely acceptable in the eighteenth century. She had relationships with married men, had a child out of marriage, lived with a man without being married, and, although she later married William Godwin whom she loved dearly, they unconventionally lived in separate apartments. When Godwin wrote his memoir about Mary after her death, the details of her love life shocked readers and ruined her public reputation for years to come, showing that society was not ready to accept women as equally as men.

In both *A Vindication of the Rights of Woman* and her unfinished novel *Maria: or, the Wrongs of Woman*, Mary compares marriage to a prison and argues that marriage as an institution controls female sexuality and reduces women to commodities.

Mary's Contribution to Feminism

Mary is sometimes described as a 'proto-feminist' (proto meaning first) or the 'mother of feminism', as she lived before the concept and term existed, but her life and work undoubtably contributed to the development of feminism many years later.

In her early book, *Thoughts on the Education of Daughters*, Mary gives her opinion on the education of children, and although there is a focus on how girls can be good wives and daughters, there is an emphasis on the importance of education, reading, good conversation and a good moral upbringing, and this is a key early feminist idea. As Mary states: 'Girls learn something of music, drawing, and geography; but they do not know enough to engage their attention, and render it an employment of the mind.'

On reading, she has a passionate view: 'A relish for reading, or any of the fine arts, should be cultivated very early in life.' She also expands on her feelings about feminine dress, hair and make-up which she had previously expressed her distaste for.

Wollstonecraft was critiquing the view of some male writers at the time, particularly Jean-Jacques Rousseau, who had some progressive ideas on education, but argued that women should be submissive to men, were natural caregivers and homemakers and were incapable of reason.

The argument that girls should receive a full education and learn skills to enable them to function independently was built on later in her seminal text *A Vindication of the Rights of Woman*.

Published in 1792, *A Vindication of the Rights of Woman: with Strictures on Political and Moral Subjects* is considered an important early work of feminist philosophy. It follows her classical liberalist beliefs that the rights of men and the rights of women are the same. Women are human beings first, and women second, and therefore should be entitled to all the same rights as men. She makes the argument that if women are to contribute fully to society, and not just be 'domestic slaves', then they should be educated, allowed to work and be financially independent:

'My main argument is built on this simple principle, that if she be not prepared by education to become the companion of man, she will stop the progress of knowledge, for truth must be common to all.'

'Strengthen the female mind by enlarging it, and there will be an end to blind obedience.'

She writes about how women are told as children that their main role is to be submissive and beautiful and to attract the attention of men, and this prevents them from achieving more in life. Whereas, it is clear that Mary wants women to be able to achieve so much more: 'Women are told from their infancy, and taught by the example of their mothers, that a little knowledge of human weakness, justly termed cunning, softness of temper, OUTWARD obedience, and a scrupulous attention to a puerile kind of propriety, will obtain for them the protection of man; and should they be beautiful, everything else is needless.'

Many years after her death, she influenced several significant writers such as Virginia Woolf, who said that Mary's voice was still being heard. Even later, she was quoted and remembered in connection with the Women's Suffrage Movement, as an 'early claimant to feminist freedom.'[1]

Wollstonecraft and Liberalism

What is Classical Liberalism?

Linked to Mary's feminist attitudes are her beliefs in liberalism and individualism. Classical liberalism is an early form of liberalism, a political philosophy that developed amongst the middle classes in the eighteenth century, which centred around individual freedoms and equal rights, maximising opportunities for individuals to grow and develop skills, and a move towards a more democratic society.[2] Although different from what we would consider equality and liberalism today, the key thinkers in the movement had radical ideas for their time.

Key Themes in Liberalism

Natural rights – Everyone is born with rights at birth. John Locke developed this theory, arguing that all humans should have the right to freedom, life and property.

Democracy – A way of governing where society has a say, through elected representation or where power is given to members of a society.

Less government control – A liberalist philosophy believes in less government control and interference in order to allow people to make their own rights and choices. Liberalists also believe in a 'free market economy', which means the markets should also operate outside of government control.

Individual freedoms – Liberal thinkers believed that the individual is the best person to make their own choices and should have the right to freedom of speech, to own property, to manage their own money and choose their own faith.

The Enlightenment and reason – The Enlightenment is closely linked to the beliefs of liberalism. The Enlightenment was an intellectual and cultural movement and a time of rapid scientific and technical discovery in seventeenth- and eighteenth-century Europe and celebrated reason, rational thought, science and logic.

Development of Mary's Liberalist Beliefs

In Newington Green, Mary met many radical free thinkers who greatly influenced her political views. This group of people were called the 'Rational Dissenters'[3], and many of the famous Dissenters such as Dr Richard Price, Joseph Johnson, and Joseph Priestley became Mary's friends and associates.[4] The Dissenters believed in Unitarianism rather than the traditional hierarchical Church of England, and had more rational views of religion.

They believed the Church of England was too strict and hierarchical; they believed in one God and Jesus as a human teacher, rather than the spiritual concept of the Holy Trinity; and they resented state control of religion and education. In response, they instead set up their own churches and educational institutions.[5] Newington Green was home to a famous Unitarian Chapel, where Dr Price preached and Mary attended sermons.

This freedom of thought was inspirational to Mary, who felt trapped as a powerless female in a male-dominated society, and responded to her own lack of education with a strong assertion that girls should be educated just as much as boys if they are to contribute fully to an equal society.

Key Liberalist Thinkers

John Locke (1632–1704) – Often referred to as the father of classical liberalism, he championed individual rights and freedoms, developed the theory of 'natural rights' and the 'social contract'.

Jean-Jacques Rousseau (1712-1778) – A key Enlightenment thinker known for his child-centred educational theories, which influenced progressive educational theory today. He believed that children should be taught depending on their own interests and not through rigid schooling, but he also had some controversial ideas about how arts and sciences had led to moral decay. Mary Wollstonecraft critiqued Rousseau heavily in her work, as he did not think girls should be educated as equally as boys.

Adam Smith (1723–1790) – Famous for his work *The Wealth of Nations* and his radical thoughts about the economy and free markets.

Dr Richard Price (1723–1791) – A philosopher and theologian, minister of the Unitarian Chapel in Newington Green. One of the first radicals Mary Wollstonecraft met, he introduced her to many more. Known for his support of the American Revolution.

Joseph Priestley (1733–1804) – A key scientific thinker, who discovered oxygen. A big thinker in the Radical Dissenters movement and promoted Unitarianism as a religion.

Thomas Paine (1737–1809) – A key political and pro-republican thinker of the eighteenth century. Though born in England, he moved to America where he published *Common Sense* in 1776, which was highly influential for American independence. His text *Rights of Man* supported French Revolution and also influenced Mary Wollstonecraft's *A Vindication of the Rights of Men*.

Joseph Johnson (1738–1809) – A bookseller and publisher who advanced liberalism through his publishing of radical texts in the eighteenth century. As well as publishing Mary's work, he published work by William Godwin and Thomas Paine.

Wollstonecraft and the French Revolution

The French Revolution was a series of events which happened from 1789 to 1799, which took France from being ruled by a monarch, King Louis XVI, to being a republican state.

Background of the French Revolution

In the late eighteenth century, King Louis XVI's excessive spending and his support of the American Revolution had nearly bankrupted France. Although there was a government with ministers, the King historically had the 'divine right to rule' and France was ruled as an absolute monarchy, meaning no one could effectively prevent the King from doing as he pleased. There were high taxes, huge social inequalities and poverty. Bad harvests and lack of money led to riots and revolts, such as the Parisian Bread Riots. The Enlightenment period and ideas circulating about freedom, rights and equality inspired the people to challenge the monarchy to have a greater say in how the country was governed.

Before the Revolution, the King summoned a meeting of the Estates General – an assembly of representatives from the people of France. The First Estate were religious figures; the Second Estate were the nobility, people with titles; and the Third Estate were supposed to represent everyone else in France. The Third Estate had more numbers but much less power in this assembly, so they broke away in June 1789 and instead formed the National Assembly – a revolutionary group formed of the ordinary people of France. This signified a loss of control by the King and started the period of the Revolution.

The National Assembly produced the *Declaration of the Rights of Man and of the Citizen* in 1789, a key civil rights document that was the foundation of the beliefs during the French Revolution. It was originally drafted by Marquis de Lafayette, who had played a role in the American Revolution, and Thomas Jefferson supported him in producing it. The declaration draws on ideas from the Enlightenment such as liberty, individualism and equal rights to all men.

The Storming of the Bastille

On 14 July 1789, the people of France broke into the Bastille Prison, rioting and killing the Governor. Seven prisoners were freed. This was a significant event for the Revolution as it marked a violent escalation of events, moving the country into outright revolution and away from compromise with the monarchy.

The Arrest of the King

Shortly after Bastille Day, a mob arrived at Versailles and the King and his family were forced to move to Paris to live in Tuileries Palace. The revolutionaries thought that the King would be more accountable to them and would lead better if he was among them in Paris, rather than enjoying court life in Versailles.

In June 1791, the King, along with his wife Marie Antoinette and their family, tried to escape Paris to Verannes in the night, aiming for the Austrian border in disguise. They were caught and returned to the Palace under house arrest. The King's attempt to escape weakened his position even more and angered the French people, who thought he was a coward and must be colluding with foreign powers, such as Austria.

In 1792, the Revolution was intensifying and revolutionaries stormed the Tuileries Palace, overwhelming the guards and setting fire to parts of the Palace and grounds. King Louis XVI was arrested on 13 August 1792 and taken to Temple, a prison fortress in Paris. The National Assembly then declared France to be a republic on 21 September and stripped the King of his titles. He was marched through the streets in December and put on trial for treason, an event which Mary Wollstonecraft witnessed when she had arrived in Paris. He was found guilty in January, and the National Convention voted on execution by the guillotine, which took place on 21 January 1793.

The Reign of Terror

After the King's death, the revolutionaries went to war with different European powers and led a bloodthirsty campaign against people accused of being traitors or counter-revolutionaries, resulting in thousands of deaths, known as The Terror. One key figure in this period was Maximilien Robespierre, an influential lawyer and member of the Committee of Public Safety, who ordered public executions for any 'enemy of France' whose philosophies differed from his own. Apparently influenced by Enlightenment ideas, Robespierre was seeking to establish Rousseau's idea of a social contract, a government formed of people with equal rights and powers, but believed he first had to eliminate anyone who was not 'virtuous' enough. He did this by terrorising his enemies in order to break down their will to resist.

Mary Wollstonecraft in France

Mary Wollstonecraft was already following the events of the French Revolution keenly, as she had published her *A Vindication on the Rights of Men* in response to Edmund Burke's anti-revolution pamphlet (more on that below), but she travelled there in the winter of 1792. She stayed in the house of a French family, and witnessed King Louis XVI passing by on the way to his trial. This event moved and disturbed her, and she wrote to Johnson: 'I can scarcely tell you why, but an association of ideas made the tears flow insensibly from my eyes, when I saw Louis sitting, with more dignity than I expected from his character, in a hackney coach going to meet death.'

Despite this shocking start, Mary seemed to enjoy life in Revolutionary Paris, meeting like-minded radicals and enjoying the more relaxed attitudes to women. Women attended clubs and societies and spoke publicly in assemblies.[6] No fault divorce had been legalised in France, and she met intellectual women in social circles with whom she identified. She attended 'salons' (social get-togethers for intellectuals) hosted by Helen Maria Williams, an English poet and writer, religious Dissenter and fellow pro-revolutionary, who was later arrested and imprisoned during the Terror. Mary wrote frequently in France, and at one point was writing a plan for education for the National Convention.

Along with other British radicals, she later became disillusioned with the Revolution and the ultra-violence of the Terror, and wrote: 'I am afraid that the morals of the people will not be much improved by the change, or the government rendered less venal.'

As the reign of terror intensified, foreigners living in Paris were put under surveillance. The English were enemies, and Mary could have been considered a spy. Mary moved to a small village outside of Paris just before many English people, including Helen Maria Williams, were arrested. She met and started a relationship with Gilbert Imlay, an American diplomat and entrepreneur, and, when realising she was pregnant, moved back to Paris. Imlay registered her as his wife to give her the protection of being married to an American, though an actual marriage never took place. Life in Paris seemed chaotic, with Mary writing of 'a round of prison visits and all too frequent news of the execution of her friends'.

She continued writing, working on her book about the French Revolution whilst she was pregnant. She posted the manuscript to Johnson in England, and the book entitled *An Historical and Moral View of the French Revolution* was published in London in 1794. The book is praised for being one of her best works, drawing on journals, articles and records of the time to present an 'accurate history of the Revolution to counteract the increasing counter-revolutionary repression and hysteria in Britain' according to academic Tom Furniss.[7]

She gave birth to Fanny Imlay in Le Havre. Imlay left Mary and their daughter and moved to England, and Mary struggled in a very cold winter of 1794-5. She followed Imlay back to London with baby Fanny, and on finding him living with an actress, attempted suicide for the first time.

The Revolution Controversy in Britain

The 'Revolution Controversy' is the name given to the intellectual and political debates which happened in Britain around the time of the French Revolution, also known as a pamphlet war. Pamphlets were quickly produced written arguments about a current issue, around the time when developments in the printing press meant that they could be mass-produced cheaply. Pamphleteers often attacked or defended an idea, producing an argument or counter-argument to advance the debate.

The French Revolution pamphlet war in Britain began when Whig MP Edmund Burke produced *Reflections on the Revolution in France* in 1790, heavily criticising the French Revolution and defending the monarchy. Burke himself wrote this in response to Dr Richard Price's sermon supporting the Revolution, which he gave in Newington Green. Burke criticised the views of many British radical thinkers and argues that the people of a country do not have the right to challenge the authority of the government or monarchy, as such actions would lead to anarchy.

Many radical writers quickly wrote a response, including Thomas Paine and William Godwin. The first response to be published was Mary Wollstonecraft, who responded with her pamphlet *A Vindication of the Rights of Men, in a Letter to the Right Honourable Edmund Burke; Occasioned by His Reflections on the Revolution in France*, also in 1790. Mary criticised Burke's gendered language and his arguments that the passivity of women would be part of a successful society, and instead presented a view of an equal society based on Enlightenment principles and progressive republican views.

Synopsis of *Mary and the Hyenas*

This synopsis contains plot spoilers

The play opens with Wollstonecraft giving birth to Mary Shelley, her second daughter, in 1797. Adult Mary Shelley is watching, and the two have a conversation about how they never had the chance to really meet: '*You will never know me. Ten days. You won't remember me. You won't remember me at all.*' What follows is the story of Mary Wollstonecraft's life, told with Mary Shelley watching and commenting on the action.

This biographical play is based on true people and events from history, presented in scenes which are labelled 'chapters'. There are also contemporary songs which punctuate and comment on the action.

Chapter One takes us back to Beverley, in North Yorkshire in 1773, when Mary is fourteen. Mary's father, Edward, comes home drunk and we see his violent nature. Mary and her mother, Elizabeth are told to pack as they are moving to London.

Chapter Two is set in London, 1774. Mary is reading when Fanny Blood arrives to meet them. Mary is in awe of Fanny, she paints and earns money for her work to support her family, and this independence is inspirational to Mary. They bond over the John Locke book Mary is reading. Mary tries to convince Fanny, and her sisters Everina and Eliza that they do not need to get married, that women can live independently.

Chapter Three moves on to 1781. Mary's mother Elizabeth is dying, and Mary is nursing her. Despite Mary being there, Elizabeth is asking for Edward, her husband, and Ned, her eldest son. Mary repeats that Ned is not coming and is not interested. Mary urges her mother to feel angry about how she has been neglected: '*Can you not be angry with how they have left us? Can you not curse them?*' Elizabeth dies, and Mary leaves angrily.

Chapter Four is set in Hackney, 1783, at Eliza and Meredith Bishop's wedding. Mary '*stages a rescue*', grabbing Eliza and taking her away from Bishop. Mary, Eliza and Everina then set up a school for girls in Newington Green.

Chapter Five sees Mary in Newington Green, 1784, where she is teaching. Fanny has joined them, and together they go to hear a sermon at the Newington Green Unitarian Church by Dr Richard Price, '*famous insurrectionary preacher. Philosopher. Beard-sporter. Rebellion-inciter.*' Fanny is coughing and we see she is unwell, suffering from tuberculosis. They talk to Dr Price and are introduced to Joseph Johnson, '*publisher, purveyor of radical thoughts and dissenting minds.*' Johnson suggests Mary write a pamphlet on the issue of female education.

In Chapter Six, the action has moved to Portugal, where Fanny moved to marry Hugh Skeys, but dies in childbirth. Mary is heartbroken, held back by the Chorus as Fanny is buried. Back at the school, Everina and Eliza tell her the school has failed. Mary decides she will go to Ireland to take a governess position.

In Chapter Seven, Mary is in Ireland in 1786 and meets her employer Lady Kingsborough, a wealthy aristocrat. Lady Kingsborough fusses over her pet dogs but does not seem to care much about her children. Mary meets Margaret Kingsborough, her pupil, who will go on to be inspired by Mary.

In Chapter Eight, Margaret and Mary talk during their lesson, and Mary asks Margaret what she wants to do in life: '*A young woman of your potential needs to see the world. See it and make up your own mind.*'

In Chapter Nine, Lady Kingsborough enters furiously, labelling Mary a radical and accusing her of encouraging defiance in Margaret, who is now refusing marriage. Mary is fired and returns to London.

Chapter Ten sees Mary publish *Thoughts on the Education Of Daughters* with Joseph Johnson.

In Chapter Eleven, Mary attends a dinner held by Joseph Johnson, where notable fellow radicals are in attendance. She discusses ideas of liberty with Paine, Johnson, Fuseli and

Godwin. Godwin suggests she is overbearing, and Mary rejects this notion, suggesting: *'Has it occurred to you, Mr Godwin, that the reason I appear 'overbearing' is simply because you are used to members of my sex folding themselves into the background and deferring to male opinion?'* She is incensed, and furiously writes *A Vindication of the Rights of Woman*.

Mary's book is published and the critics respond harshly, calling the work 'outrageous' and 'preposterous' (Chapter Twelve). Johnson suggests she relocates to Paris, where a new world is being formed through the Revolution.

In Paris in Chapter Thirteen, Mary meets Helen Williams, a fellow radical, and joins one of her salons. Helen introduces her to Gilbert Imlay, an American diplomat. They flirt and begin a whirlwind relationship. Mary questions whether she can change what she believes and asks him to assure her it is a real relationship. The scene ends with Mary showing Mary Shelley that she is now pregnant.

In Chapter Fourteen, Mary and Imlay argue about him leaving her, amidst the increasingly tense situation in Paris. They agree to register as married to protect Mary, as the English were under suspicion.

The Reign of Terror begins (Chapter Fifteen) and Mary is heavily pregnant, cold and hungry. She meets Marguerite, who becomes her maid and delivers her baby, named Fanny. Mary, Marguerite and Fanny get on the ship to go to Scandinavia to try and find Imlay's treasure, through Marguerite tells her it is mad, and Imlay himself would go if he cared. Imlay sends Mary a letter, saying he is returning to London, and Mary feels upset and rejected. Marguerite comforts her, saying he is not worthy of her, and they return to London.

In Chapter Sixteen, back in London (1795), Mary goes to Imlay's house. She confronts him about his other woman, and he ends the relationship, saying he is a free man and will not be made to feel guilty. He accuses Mary of harassing him.

Desperate and heartbroken, Mary goes to Putney Bridge and considers ending her life. She battles with her inner conflict, hearing the voices of her critics. Mary Shelley tries to stop her, saying she must continue to fight. Mary jumps, and Mary Shelley pulls her out alive, cradling her body.

In Chapter Seventeen, Mary recovers, and Marguerite, Fanny and Johnson are all around her bedside. She explains that she felt overwhelmed and did not think she could go on. Her friends support her, and she resolves to tell the rest of the story.

Godwin comes to visit Mary at Johnson's (Chapter Eighteen, 1796). Godwin admits he enjoyed her *Letters from Sweden, Norway and Denmark* and asks if they could be friends, perhaps developing into something more. Mary is surprised but considers it. They agree to a '*a marriage of equals*', Mary will not stop working, and Godwin will support her writing.

In Chapter Nineteen, Mary and Godwin are contently writing together, Mary is heavily pregnant. It is the end.

In the Epilogue, Mary asks her daughter if anything did actually change, '*Was it worth it? Do we change anything? Anything at all? Tell me. Tell me please.*' Mary Shelley replies: '*So much. So so much.*' We see various women after Mary who have been influenced by her, who have fought for equality and change. Mary started the revolution which is still going on.

This synopsis was prepared from the rehearsal draft of the script and may differ from the final version of the play.

Themes and Topics

Family and Motherhood

Several family relationships are explored in the play, beginning with the mother-daughter relationship between Mary Wollstonecraft and Mary Shelley, which frames the narrative.

Despite never knowing each other, Mary Shelley was inspired by her mother's work, and this play imagines the conversations they would have had.

Mary Wollstonecraft's family life is explored in detail, and we see the relationship she has with both of her parents and her sisters.

Her father is abusive and dismissive of Mary, calling her an '*an impudent little slattern*' and physically assaulting her, when she is trying to protect her mother. Mary stands up for herself and her mother but is ultimately overruled and overpowered by her father. This reflects the patriarchal society of the time, which Edwards abuses. Men did have more rights, and were the legal guardians of the children, which is why Eliza must leave her baby when she leaves Meredith Bishop, and the baby subsequently dies.

On her death bed, Mary's mother Elizabeth calls only for Ned, her son, despite Mary being there to care for her. Mary begs her mother to see her, but Elizabeth calls for Ned, her '*darling baby boy*', and Edward, her abusive husband. Mary questions what hope her mother had for the three girls when they were born and begs her mother to be angry for her waste of a life. Elizabeth tells Mary she was always jealous, and was never a kind girl.

Despite the lack of love and care Mary received from her own parents, she is a loving mother to Fanny, taking her with her to Scandinavia and vowing to raise her without Imlay's help: '*My little girl, that I have loved and grown and cherished and fed and held and bathed and fought for.*'

Although women were expected to have children, pregnancy and childbirth came with risk and danger for women, due to poor standards of hygiene and lack of proper maternity care in the eighteenth century. In the play, Fanny dies in childbirth, and her child dies too; Eliza's child dies after she leaves; and Mary dies ten days after childbirth, after the doctor introduced an infection when treating her. Mary had a retained placenta after giving birth and developed an infection and a lack of medical knowledge, pain relief, antibiotics and sterilised equipment, led to a painful and slow, but avoidable, death for Mary.

Questions for students to consider:

- How has the concept of family changed since Mary's time?
- How have conditions for pregnancy and childbirth changed and improved since the eighteenth century?
- What legal changes have been put into place now to protect parents and children?
- Why did women not have legal rights to their children in the eighteenth century?

Education

Advocating for education for girls was central to Mary's work. As well as working as a governess she set up schools for girls in Islington and Newington Green, and Eliza and Everina set up a further school in Ireland after Mary's death.

Before the seventeenth century, girls received some education, but this was only provided at home and was connected to class and wealth for a long time. Girls from wealthy families would have a governess, like Mary, and would be taught reading, writing and skills to help them be attractive as a wife, such as music, French and needlework.

From the seventeenth century onwards, boarding schools were opened for girls, but again this was for wealthy families, and

girls were not allowed to go to university. When they were
admitted to university, women did not receive degrees, only a
Certificate of Proficiency. Oxford and Cambridge Universities
did not start awarding degrees to women until 1920 and 1948,
respectively. It was not until 1880, and the introduction of
the Education Act, that all girls and boys had to go to school
between the ages of five and ten.

Mary Wollstonecraft believed that for women to contribute fully
to society they needed to be educated. She wrote *Thoughts on
the Education of Daughters* after working as a governess in
Ireland. She was critical of girls spending too much time on
their appearance, and argued that reading is vital for opening the
mind. In the play, she opens a school with the aim of *'teaching
girls to cultivate their minds and bodies, to be able to speak for
themselves, articulate themselves on their own terms.'*

Questions for students to consider:

- To what extent are educational opportunities equal for girls now?
- Is education the same for everyone around the world?
- What do you think still needs to improve to make education more equal?
- Why do you think Mary's views were seen as so radical at the time?

Relationships

Several types of relationships are explored in the play. We see
the family relationships between Mary, her sisters and parents,
but lots of close friendships and romantic relationships, such as:

Mary and Fanny – Mary is besotted with Fanny when they
meet, and is *'transfixed'*. Fanny is described as *'the love of her
life'*, and though not explicitly stated, it is suggested that Mary
has deep, romantic feelings for Fanny. Mary does not want
Fanny to marry Hugh Skeys and wants to care for her instead.

When it is clear that Fanny is unwell, Mary suggests she goes to Portugal where it is warmer. Mary is devastated by Fanny's death, and names her baby after her best friend.

Mary and Marguerite – Marguerite is a loving and loyal friend in Mary's life, and stays with her until the end of her life. She tries to warn Mary off Imlay, saying that if he cared for them at all, he would not have sent Mary to Scandinavia with her baby.

Mary and Imlay – Imlay is Mary's first love, and even though she is cautious at first, she completely falls for his charm and is betrayed by him. He treats their relationship as a meaningless fling and uses her to try and do his work in Scandinavia for him. She is left with baby Fanny when Imlay moves on and he starts a relationship with an actress. He is romantic and charming to begin with, and later accuses her of '*harassing*' him and driving him away. This devastates Mary, and she attempts to end her life.

Mary and Fuseli – Fuseli is portrayed as a flirtatious man, who is married but makes several suggestive comments to Mary. Even though he is willing to be promiscuous, he still fears scandal in public.

Mary and Johnson – Johnson is a loyal friend and advocate of Mary's work. He gives her a job as an editor and writer, and provides accommodation for her, allowing her to live and work independently, which was rare for women at the time. He publishes her work and encourages her to write throughout her life.

Mary and Godwin – When they first meet, Mary and Godwin clash, as Mary assumes he is another misogynistic man who is trying to oppress women, but they find they agree on issues such as marriage. Godwin comes to admire Mary's work, and proposes they start a relationship after she is back from Paris. Because of Imlay, Mary is wary at first, but agrees to a relationship if she can retain her independence. Godwin is kind and respectful, and they live peacefully together, living in separate apartments where they can both write. Godwin is heartbroken at Mary's death and raises Fanny as his own child.

Questions for students to consider:

- Which of the relationships in Mary's life had a positive effect on her, and which were negative?
- To what extent do you think Mary's early relationships affected her later life?
- What were the differences between Mary's romantic relationships with Imlay and Godwin?
- How does Mary's relationship with Johnson shape her life?
- If Fanny was not unwell and had not died in childbirth, what do you think her and Mary's future would have been?

Mental Health

Mary attempted suicide twice in her life, and frequently wrote about her mental ill health in her letters. In the play, we see Mary jump into the River Thames, after being rejected by Imlay and experiencing depressive thoughts: '*I wasn't sure I could do it anymore. I couldn't, I, I wasn't, and I thought Fanny would be better without me. I thought maybe everything would just be better without me.*' The inequalities for women would have exacerbated Mary's situation, given that she was a single mother at the time. In the song, 'Strong Woman', she sings about feeling she has the weight of the world on her shoulders, trying to be strong and exceptional, but still wanting to be held.

Eliza also suffered with mental ill health, experiencing what we would now know as postnatal depression, or PND. There was very little understanding of mental health at the time, especially for women, who would have been regarded as being 'hysterical' or suffering from a 'nervous disorder'. Even up to the twentieth century, people who experienced mental ill health were not treated with care or respect. There was no understanding of therapy, and treatment was extreme. People were institutionalised in mental asylums, and often remained there for the rest of their lives, shut away from society.

Even today, there can still be a stigma in regards to mental health, and other factors affect our mental health greatly. This is called intersectionality – where factors of life overlap and create more disadvantage. For example, people who experience poverty are more likely to experience mental ill health, and people with mental ill health are more likely to encounter substance abuse.

Creative Exercises for Teachers

These exercises can be used to introduce students to the themes and narrative of *Mary and the Hyenas* before they read or see the play. You could pick and choose from these activities or put them together for a longer workshop. Some activities are suitable for all key stages and some activities are more challenging and designed for KS5.

Content warning: The themes and synopsis contain detailed information about death, grief and mental ill health which may be triggering, please ensure this is appropriate for your group before sharing.

Exploring the Themes

Put students into groups and give each group one of the themes from these resources. Ask students to read the information and to research their theme and present back to the rest of the class. This could be done as a flip-learning task, where students take away the theme and research it as homework before coming back and presenting it in class.

Understanding the Synopsis

Put students into groups and give each group a copy of the full synopsis from these resources. Ask students to read the synopsis aloud, taking turns in reading to develop oracy. Then, ask students to break down the synopsis into key moments, which could be done using the 'chapters' of the play, and to write these on to a large piece of paper. This helps students to digest the synopsis and simplifies it for younger learners.

Still Images

Using the key moments from the synopsis, ask students to create a still image of each key moment. Encourage them to use levels, space, physical contact and to consider their body language and facial expressions. The images could be performed to music to create an emotive piece of physical theatre.

Performing Mary's Words

Take an extract from Wollstonecraft's *Thoughts on the Education of Daughters*, below, and ask students to physicalise and stage this in groups.

Using the text, they should find creative ways of bringing this to life on stage: they could use choral speaking, rap, song, music, still images, gestures, choreography or multimedia. Ensure students do not change the words, but the section could be shortened for younger students.

Extract from *Thoughts on the Education of Daughters*, 1787

It is an old, but a very true observation, that the human mind must ever be employed. A relish for reading, or any of the fine arts, should be cultivated very early in life; and those who reflect can tell, of what importance it is for the mind to have some resource in itself, and not to be entirely dependent on the senses for employment and amusement.

If it unfortunately is so, it must submit to meanness, and often to vice, in order to gratify them. The wisest and best are too much under their influence; and the endeavouring to conquer them, when reason and virtue will not give their sanction, constitutes great part of the warfare of life. What support, then, have they who are all senses, and who are full of schemes, which terminate in temporal objects?

Reading is the most rational employment, if people seek food for the understanding, and do not read merely

to remember words; or with a view to quote celebrated
authors, and retail sentiments they do not understand
or feel. Judicious books enlarge the mind and improve
the heart, though some, by them, 'are made coxcombs
whom nature meant for fools.'

Designing Mary

Ask students to research clothing and fashion in eighteenth-century England and design a costume for Mary in this production. They could make a mood board of ideas before they produce their design. They could choose to make her costume traditional, or it could be stylised and could borrow influences from different time periods. Ask students to consider how they can convey Mary's personality and attitudes through her costume, hair and make-up. You could choose to show students the various portraits of Mary from her lifetime, and the front cover of this book, or let them design their own ideas first.

Imagined Meetings

The play is framed by an imagined conversation between Mary Wollstonecraft and her daughter Mary Shelley. In groups, students could stage an imagined scene between Mary Wollstonecraft and some of the future characters mentioned in the play who are inspired by her: Elizabeth Barrett Browning, George Eliot, Millicent Fawcett or Virginia Woolf. Students could do research on each of these characters before the session, or you could provide biographical details. If this feels too challenging, students could imagine they meet Mary Wollstonecraft themselves and devise a scene in which they talk to her. This could be done as a TV chat show or podcast interview.

Endnotes

1. In *Westminster Gazette* 16 October 1906 https://blog.britishnewspaperarchive.co.uk/2024/03/27/legacy-of-mary-wollstonecraft, accessed: 03 December 2024.
2. https://iea.org.uk/publications/research/classical-liberalism-a-primer, accessed: 03 December 2024.
3. Smith, V. *Rational Dissenters in Late Eighteenth-Century England: An Ardent Desire of Truth*, 2021.
4. Tomalin, C. *The Life and Death of Mary Wollstonecraft*. 1974.
5. Ibid.
6. Kirkley L. *Mary Wollstonecraft: Cosmopolitan*. 2022.
7. Furniss, T. 'Mary Wollstonecraft's French Revolution' in *The Cambridge Companion to Mary Wollstonecraft*, ed. Claudia L. Johnson. 2006. p.68.

Books

Memoirs of the Author of A Vindication of the Rights of Woman, William Godwin. 1798.

Romantic Outlaws: The Extraordinary Lives of Mary Wollstonecraft & Mary Shelley, Charlotte Gordon. Random House, 2015.

The Cambridge Companion to Mary Wollstonecraft, ed. Claudia L. Johnson. Cambridge University Press, 2006.

The Life and Death of Mary Wollstonecraft, Claire Tomalin. London, Weidenfeld & Nicolson, 1974.

Websites

The Wollstonecraft Society: https://www.wollstonecraftsociety.org/, accessed 03 December 2024.